T0194448

# Journey to SPIRITUAL SELF

Internal Empowerment

AQUALMA S. Y. MURRAY, M.A.

Balboa Press books may be ordered through booksellers or by contacting:

Balboa Press
A Division of Hay House
1663 Liberty Drive
Bloomington, IN 47403
www.balboapress.com
1 (877) 407-4847



Print information available on the last page.

ISBN: 978-1-9822-2383-0 (sc)
ISBN: 978-1-9822-2385-4 (hc)
ISBN: 978-1-9822-2384-7 (e)

Library of Congress Control Number: 2019904932

Balboa Press rev. date: 07/10/2019

**INSPIRING OR WHAT!**

**THE JOURNEY TO SPIRITUAL SELF—A Spiritual Biography**

SPIRITUALLY WHOLE AND COMPLETE

# Contents

# Acknowledgements

In order to acknowledge the many people and experiences that have brought me to this point in my life and enabled me to finally complete this book, I have to first give thanks to the Most High who has protected and guided me along this journey to a place of spiritual knowing—thank you, my blessed mother and father God.

I am also truly grateful to my earth mother, Bernice Eugenie Campbell Murray, God rest her soul, who loved me so dearly and made me feel so precious. My mother showed a deep respect, understanding and acceptance of me, even when she disagreed with my views or actions, which has taught me to hold an appreciation and value for others who may be similar or different to me.

My father and brothers, (the Murrays), proud and confident in their sense of togetherness and a belief in their accumulative strength allowed me to feel special and valued, so much so that they were extremely overprotective of me, which although hindering me at times has also allowed me to safely become who I am today, a very strong, powerful, yet humble, independent and calm black woman.

I want to express a big thank you to the Historian, Dr Josef Ben-Jochannah, who my niece, Laverne and I met in the 90s while on holiday in Egypt. Dr Ben-Jochannah kindly took time out of his very busy schedule to meet with us and he gave me guidance on writing this book, he advised me to include at least four pictures as this will make the book more interesting. I followed his advice. God rest his soul. I am truly grateful for his time, knowledge and wisdom.

There are a number of other special people in my life, who gave me encouragement and support as I took many years to write this book. I want to thank my dearest son Parez-Jade Murray, who we refer to as PJ, for his consistent support and encouragement in helping me to remain motivated in the task of writing and training others. PJ has always been able to see the big picture and knew, somehow, what was worth holding on to and what to let go of, and he so skilfully perceived the hidden future benefits in all adverse situations. My son PJ gently reminded me that the writing of this book would assist so many others.

To my dear friend Atienda, an intelligent, articulate, strong black man who painstakingly would phone me and remind me that the writing of this book was indeed my ambition and that I needed to continue writing, in spite of my very busy life. His partner Yaa, a highly ambitious woman, a skilled lecturer in the art of writing, with a deep understanding of what allows women to feel nurtured and empowered, who kindly read the first draft of this book and gave me constructive direction.

Very recently I found the love of my life, Israle, we got married in 2017 and he has patiently read parts of the book and helped with the graphics, he also gently encouraged me to keep on going and gave me the final push to complete this task.

I am so very grateful to my dear cousin Lorraine, who painstakingly read, edited and reviewed this book in order to make it into the product that it now is. Thank you very much.

And finally, to all the people who allowed to me to get close to their lives through attending my empowerment workshops and taking part in individual spiritual counselling so that I could understand and share how the inner energy that we all share works in so many wonderful and different ways, to guide, support and help us to grow or not, as the case may be.

**The Journey to Spiritual Self**
**(The Path to a Place of Knowing)**

# Introduction

What is the purpose of life? Could it be about being available to help others or finding out who we really are? We are about to explore some of what happens in life and how we can ensure that those experience work for us.

I perceive myself as an intelligent, educated, warm, friendly and humble woman, who is keen to assist and support others. I have spent many years wondering why people suffer and what are the benefits of all the horrendous experiences some of us must endure. I think I now know some of the answer to this profound question.

This book is about the reasons that people struggle and the path to less pain and suffering through positive thinking and the connection with spirit. I will also discuss the power of positive thinking and methods towards enhancing our life experiences.

I will be sharing some life experiences as a tool to help you understand how I have overcome and assisted others in overcoming some of life's most testing challenges.

I will talk of my personal experience of sexual abuse as a small child and how I have spent my working life as a probation officer, residential social worker and now work as a Local Authority Designated Child Protection Officer (LADO), investigating professionals who pose a risk of harm to children. I will describe how I have used my pain as a child to understand the issue of children's and adult's mental health issues and how I have delivered training to a wide range of professionals who work with children.

I will discuss the issue of converting adversity into prosperity.

We will explore the avenues to living a content and happy life and experiencing amazing self-achievements, comfort and peace.

# Foreword

In order to help the reader understand how I have come to embrace spirituality and to give insight into my journey, I need to tell you a little about me. I was born in 1961, mother tells me that I was a slim baby weighing 7lbs and that I was born feet first, in a hospital in Kensington, London. My mother named me Sandra Yvonne Murray. It became apparent very early on that I had great difficulty learning to read as did my brothers, but I was determined to master this skill and I recall being of primary school age and picking up a book given to me by a teacher as homework and I would ask my brother, Leighton, to tell me what word I was trying to read. I went back to him for every word in one sentence and he patiently told me the word. Then at nine years old I wanted to write a love letter to a boy in school and sat there at the table while my mother prepared food in the adjacent kitchen and I would shout to her 'Mum how do you spell love', 'How do you spell…?' etc, etc, etc and she told me. I learnt to read at the age very close to leaving primary school and did not discover that I am dyslexic until I had achieved my social work diploma and became a probation officer. One of my managers in a London Probation office said to me 'you speak very well, but your spelling is a bit off maybe you should get tested for dyslexia,' so I paid several hundred pounds to be tested. The psychologist who assessed me commented that he was surprised that I had achieved so much academically, but warned me never to fly a plane. I have gone on to achieve a Master's in Advanced Social Work and a post qualifying award in Social work, passing with merit. I have a diploma in counselling survivors of childhood sexual abuse and I am an ordained Interfaith Minister. More recently I have collaborated with other authors and written and published a chapter about protecting children from online abuse in a book for counsellors and therapists. Who would have thought this little black girl, who grew up in poverty and had other childhood challenges; including being unable to read until quite late in childhood, would ever have achieved so much academically, emotionally and spiritually?

Throughout all my childhood the name Sandra never really felt like mine and in my teenage years I would refer to myself as Janna or something else, as I never really felt like the name given to me at birth ever really suited me. Maybe I wanted to separate myself from that name due to my painful childhood experiences. I was always a deep thinker with an imagination that was just out of this world. My mother would refer to me as melancholy as I would often day dream and had the most morbid scenarios that I would talk to her about such as 'Mum what would life be like if we were not really here and this life was just a dream and we woke up and discovered that we did not have this family we felt so connected to?' My mother thought I was a bit morbid and very melodramatic. Indeed as a child I was, but as I grew up I became more and more logical in my thinking and needed explanations and answers to the wonders of life which lead me to reading a great deal and indulging in debate with others about life after death, the struggle of poverty, what is the meaning of love, and should we really fear God. My family were good at holding debates and my mother and brothers would often sit around discussing a number of topics. Once we discussed the existence of ghosts and what if we were the ghosts, but just not conscious of it. How interesting that would be?

I became intrigued with meditation and relating to spirituality without conforming to a specific religion. As much as I wanted to belong to a particular faith, I never felt like I belonged, or I didn't like the way women were treated in those groups. I kept seeking spiritual experiences that would include me without asking me to sign up to a specific way of being in order to belong. It was during a meditation workshop that I discovered my new and current name. We were asked to sit quietly and listen to sweet soothing music with our eyes closed. I went into a lovely warm dream whereby I could hear running water and then saw in my mind's eye a little African woman passing water from hand to hand. Her back was to me and the water flowed in front her. As she stretched out her hands, she caught the water and passed it from one hand to the other and it looked like a rainbow of water that she was moving from hand to hand. I recall asking her 'what are you doing?' and she turned her head towards me and said 'Shhh.', with a finger over her lips, 'You must learn to listen to the silence'. I remember thinking, how do you listen to silence. I then asked her 'Who are you?' and she said, 'The name is Aqualma', she spelt it out A-q-u-a-l-m-a. To my surprise when I came out of the meditation, I remembered the spelling, being dyslexic that was quite an achievement for me. I thought this little African woman must be a guide of some sort, so I wrote the name down, and did not think much about it. Then one day as I was watching television there was a woman called Aquilla and I thought oh she has a name similar to mine. At that point I wondered if the name was meant to be mine and as the days passed I became convinced that it should be. I officially took on the name and went to a solicitor who drew up papers declaring that my name was now Aqualma Sandra Yvonne Murray. I have since discovered that the name Aqualma consists of two Latin words Aqua meaning water and Alma being spiritual mother, indeed my son tells me that since changing my name I am less confronting in the face of injustice and more peaceful in my protest when I feel I need to complain or object to how I have been treated or served in a public setting. I was also told by a Ghanaian student that I had the pleasure of tutoring that the name Aqualma is similar to a Ghanaian name which would be chosen for a child if the family had struggled to have a baby and was then blessed with a child. That child would be called Aqualma to say thank you Lord. My name feels like a blessing and I would like everything about my life to say thank you to the source that nourishes me.

This book is about understanding why we go through what we do and how to make every experience, good or bad, work for us. What a bold statement, and many would say that if I understood many of the horrific things that people had to endure, I would be less hasty to make such a statement. Indeed, at times, I wonder why this experience on earth is so terrifying and painful for so much of the time.

To illustrate this, I'll tell you what happened just three days after arriving in Jamaica in 2013, with the intention of seeing my ailing, elderly uncle, who had recently undergone brain surgery to remove a swelling and a blood clot from the right frontal lobe of his brain. Uncle Phineas, at the age of 85, had survived the surgery but required ongoing hospitalisation in order to heal. He was alive and growing stronger every day. Myself and my two cousins C and Bonny, took the nine-and-a-half hour plane flight to Kingston, Jamaica where we were to be met by my eldest brother Clement, my mother's first son. My cousin C was met by her father and went off with him. My cousin Bonny and I waited for a short while to be met by my brother Clement who got the car and off we went on the two-hour drive to my Aunt J's home. As we drove in the warm night air we admired the improvements to the roads in Jamaica. The main road had been tremendously improved. It was smooth and wide with bright cat's eyes, and there were two brand new toll booths. Clement spoke of how proud we should be of all that had been achieved over the past few years in relation to the infrastructure of Jamaica—it was noted that we have a long way to go but things are looking up. We drove the long pretty road for some two hours, happily chatting away and feeling good to be in lovely Jamaica. Clement and I were in the front of the car while Bonny relaxed in the back which did not prevent him from frequently engaging in the conversation about the way Jamaica use to be and how things had changed.

Then we got to Clement's home area, a nice little quiet place in Manchester, commonly known as the country part of Jamaica. The roads were quiet with just a few stores and bars open and a small number of people walking or riding their bikes around in the dusk of the evening when it was now just getting dark. Without informing Bonny and I, Clement had decided to stop at his home so that we could say hi to his wife Ros, before going on to Aunt J's home which was a further thirty-minute drive. So we drove down the dark, untreated road, over big rocks, ditches, bumps and gulley's, very slowly and carefully until we got to Clement's gated but unlocked front door. I quickly got out of the car and went into the house and hugged, my sister-in-law, Ros, with my cousin Bonny very closed behind me. As cousin Bonny greeted Ros, I turned back out of the gate and saw my brother busily looking into the car for his phone that had slipped underneath the front seat. I joined him in the search and very quickly found his Blackberry phone under the back area of the driver's seat.

Having handed the phone to Clement, we started to make our way back into the house, at which point three unknown men appeared at the gated entrance and spoke in a very authoritarian tone, saying, "We are looking for someone, a short man who has killed a man down the road." We had hardly answered them to say that no such person lived there nor was such a person in the house, when they quickly ushered us all into the house, saying 'Get in, go in the house now.' Two of the men had their hands on their trouser waists as if they had guns or other weapons there, the third man quickly brandished a long, broad knife. On entering the house, one of the men stepped forward and did all the talking. He was quite menacing and aggressive and asked us if we had guns on us, still brandishing the knife. I was terrified but, somehow, I remembered my social work training about diffusing aggression. Unfortunately, they were near the door and we were not. The first thing the social work training told us was to stay near to the escape route, the door, which we were not. So, I sat on the sofa in order not to appear threatening and asked them what they wanted, however the main aggressor was focused on my cousin Bonny who stood silently in the middle of the room and did not answer when the aggressor kept asking him who he was. So, I answered and was very careful not to indicate that we had just come off a plane and arrived in Jamaica, but without lying I said he comes from down the road, where his mother lives, this is not the man you are looking for. Then one of them took my handbag, which I had placed beside me on the black leather sofa where I sat. He threw the contents on the chair, then went in my purse and took all the money out. While that was happening, the aggressor was physically attacking my cousin Bonny with a big, long sharp kitchen knife. Without thinking, I rushed over to Bonny and got in between him and the aggressor, shouting, "Leave him alone, he has nothing for you." I pulled at the back of the aggressor's neatly pressed white T-shirt, while he wrestled with Bonny to take money that he had in his pocket, hitting him in the head with the back of the long knife. Once the aggressor had prised the money from my cousin, his attention was turned towards me as I continued to try and get in between him and my cousin. The aggressor, quickly spun around and stood firmly opposite me, holding the long sharp knife, raised above his head, and said to me in no uncertain terms, "Lady, back off, back off lady." I saw the knife raised above me most of all. I heard his voice and realised that I had placed myself at great risk, so very quickly, I did as I was told. I backed away, just a little bit, trying my best not to show any fear and attempting to act as normally as possible and kept talking. My sister-in-law shouted, "Look they have taken the money from your purse." I begged the man who still had his right hand placed on his trouser pocket, to give me back my money, as he held his other hand high in the air with my three hundred pounds, tightly grasped between his fingers triumphantly, like it was a trophy of great achievement. All three men took what they could from us and quickly left. The main aggressor with the knife stated, in a strong Jamaican accent "We don't come to hurt nobody, stay inside and don't leave the house." They left us feeling shocked, stunned and somewhat shaken. Even though we saw the car of the three robbers drive away we remained in that house as instructed by the aggressor for at least 10 minutes, under the guise of trying to phone the police who never responded to their emergency number that we called so many times.

At that point I began to feel angry and frustrated at the inadequate and feeble infrastructure of the Jamaican Police Constabulary and the lack of a sufficient emergency service. I also felt scared and worried about remaining in the space where we had been so violated by bullyish strangers who felt they had the right to take so much from us without regard for our needs or wellbeing. Most of all I wanted to get out of that house as it now felt like an unsafe place to be. So as the police were not answering their phones, I stated to my brother, his wife and my cousin, in a very assertive tone, that we should drive down the road to the local police station and report the matter. All agreed it was the right thing to do. Leaving Clement's wife in the house with her elderly brother, Bonny, Clement and I left for the Police station. On arrival we stepped out of the car and walked towards the lonely Police station. The night was now coming down, but the air was still warm. Families and individuals were either at home or behind closed doors, leaving the roads quiet, with only the chatter and banter that could be heard from the policemen and women who were on duty in the little, local, Jamaican, country police station. The police station was very well lit and for the first time since the robbery I felt safe.

We reported the crime after I expressed my anger and frustration to the officer that they did not answer the emergency number that we attempted to call several times. I felt the tears well up in my eyes. The upper part of my body curved over, while my legs felt weak and I could feel an enormous sound reaching up from the inner core of my body. A tremendous wailing sound attempted to come out of my wide open mouth, so I quickly stifled it with my hand. I cried, but only for a moment, as I felt I needed to be strong for my brother and my cousin and to ensure that I reported the crime accurately. Tears hardly ever come easily to me, yet I have never felt such rage and fear all at once, culminating in a desire to just scream and cry out loud. As usual, I managed to contain myself. The Detective Constable who was in charge that night invited us to take a seat and the slowly and methodically took our statements, but nothing ever came of the investigation and no one has ever been apprehended.

As the hours and days passed, I realised just how close we had come to death and recalled how others had died under similar circumstances, right there in Jamaica. It is commonly known in Jamaica that robbers will kill their victims in order not to be identified. But we were alive and not seriously, physically injured. It took a long time for the shock and numb feeling to pass and then every face I saw looked like the aggressor and the other robbers. And the worst part was the constant reliving of the story in my head over and over again.

I am grateful that I am in a position to retell this story and that I have life, health and strength. I ask myself where is the blessing in this situation, did someone need that money more than we did or was this an opportunity to understand this kind of fear and distress in order to be of more use to others? I imagine time will tell. This was a bad experience and I am hoping some good will come out of it. If it does, before the book is concluded, I will tell you about it. The one lesson I think I have learnt from this experience thus far is that one can be vulnerable, strong and courageous all at the same time and that this is fine. The feeling of intense fear, however, can impact on your physiology to such a degree your heart palpitates beyond control, your ability to think or not think about things feels out of control and your sense of security is non-existent. Fear triggers a sense of annihilation and robs you of the ability to combat this which leaves one feeling stuck in the middle of that place of stunned numbness with a desire to run as fast as you can, but none of these two things can happen while your body is constantly fighting for at least one of these things to happen. The feeling of fear is a like an internal hurricane swirling around the inside one's body, busting with destructive action, yet contained within thick strong walls of the body which don't bend to accommodate it and just won't let it go. All the mind can do while the body is trapped in this turmoil of fear, is wait for the hurricane to burn itself out or claim dominion over the body and mind, leaving them both unable to fulfil their task.

When gripped with such intense fear the only hope of survival is to have access to something over and above the body and mind that can assist one in dealing with the out of control feelings and the overpowering sense of possibly no longer existing. Spirit has the capacity to dwell within the body and externally at the same time and can therefore act as the fluid, flexible, bendable substance that can hold the bridge between the turmoil felt inside when fear sets in and the rigid structure of the body that refuses to let fear out. Spirit is the ultimate negotiator that allows the mind to know that there is hope over and above the emotional, physical and intellectual experience of enduring and/or intense fear.

We will explore the power within and how connection with the law of the universe may impact on our lives. We will also consider the connection with our inner spirit by looking at the correct, application of that connection of spirit. Then we will look at the unity, of body and spirit, considering how this can enhance our wellbeing which may positively impact on the future of each individual, including ourselves.

I hope this will be an amazing journey for you the reader, similar to the one I often experience; however, the good times are not constant, and there is a strength in managing the bad times as well. As I share these thoughts with you, I am also growing and therefore also looking forward to this journey.

Some of the information in this book will be hard to believe and other parts might seem a little far-fetched, but I share these true experiences with you to let you know that there are very many different phenomena in this world, some good and some bad. It is our task to seek the good and eliminate the bad. Just as the body does every time, we consume food or drink.

I will talk of my childhood and many of the experiences that caused me to question my faith and some that strengthened my faith in a higher power than myself. In order to put this journey into context, we will discuss some original traditional beliefs held by those in Africa, the Caribbean and New Zealand, amongst other parts of the world.

Throughout the pages to follow I shall share with you some true life experiences of myself, my family and others in order to explore and evidence the presence and power of spirit, the ultimate source, God, Allah or any other name that it is known by, as well as the amazing gifts that are on offer to us all from the Most High every single day.

I will look at the journey to knowing our true selves and how the pains and pleasures we experience on the way help or hinder that process. We will debate the meaning and purpose of spirit, in particular by looking at how this universal force can heal or make sense of our past and also guide us to a fruitful future.

I shall suggest some empowerment exercises you can try that might assist you in connecting to spirit and developing inner positiveness.

It is my wish that this book act as a catalyst to greater and deeper self-exploration for the reader that may bring you to a place of happiness and peace. This will help us to make this world a better and more comfortable place for all to live in. There is so much for us to do, and to complete our life roles successfully we first need to know how to be, with ourselves and with others.

Our purpose on this earth is multifaceted, so we need to be gentle with ourselves as we go through the many changes that we need to in order to be able to fulfil our life purposes.

The fact that you are reading the words of these pages means that you are now ready to take the next step in this wonderful and amazing journey to spiritual self-discovery and ultimate empowerment.

## Who am I?

I was born in London to Jamaican parents and brought up by my mother and father, mainly in the area of North West London, England.

I came into this world three weeks after my mother's dear sister, Aunt Daisy, died. Aunt Daisy was said to be the planner in the family, the one who would speak her mind and ensure that arrangements for trips and outings were all in order; she would sort things out. I have only ever seen one picture of Aunt Daisy when she was in her twenties, gathered with a number of finely dressed people at another relative's wedding. The picture is really old and was probably originally black and white but was coloured by a skilled photographer who reproduced the photo. Aunt Daisy was slim and had fine, sharp facial features, her hair was curled, and she had the sweetest expression of contentment and happiness on her face.

Yes indeed, I am very similar in character and facial expression to my dear unknown Aunt Daisy. My parents migrated to England in the late fifties, leaving Aunt Daisy and other relatives behind, so they communicated via posted letters that often took weeks to arrive. In the last letter that Aunt Daisy wrote, she said to my mother, "Don't worry, this time you will have a girl child."

I was born on a normal summer's day in July of 1961—in fact, I was born at night, exactly one minute to midnight on a Friday, and I am one of six children born to my mother and father. I have an older half-brother who was raised in Jamaica and still resides there. He is my mother's son. Within our culture, the term half-brother is not usually used as we believe that as long as one of our parents is also the other's parent then he is as much a brother as any other child. My brother in Jamaica and I speak at least every few months on the phone, and when I visit Jamaica, I stay with him for part of the time. My father also had a son before he was married, and we met him later on in Jamaica when we visited. Unfortunately, he had an accident at work and later died of his injuries at the age of approximately forty, leaving several children and a wife.

I am the only girl in the immediate family and have three brothers in England older than me and two younger brothers. Sadly, the brother born before me died in a car accident some twenty years ago. Winny was an interesting character. He was the joker and protector in the family and could always be relied upon to sit and listen if any of us ever had a problem. If possible, he would fix that problem or simply offer words of comfort. My father had a son before he was married, as did my mother. My father's son Adolphus died as a young man, but Clement remains in Jamaica. We are a close family and very concerned with each of our activities. My father was a quiet man, who simply went to work and returned home every evening. He liked cars and watching shows about animals, especially wild animals, and he also enjoyed watching boxing, I once took him and two uncles to watch Frank Bruno fight. That was great, but the fight was over in a matter of minutes, as Frank Bruno was at the top of his game at that time, but we saw several other boxers, which was good. My father was housebound in his latter days and cared for by an older brother of mine all the time. Dad spent his time in a world of dreams, often talking out loud to himself, where I think he was reliving his life experiences and creating the life experiences he never had. Over the past few years Dad's hearing had failed him, but he refused to wear a hearing aid. He also suffered with Alzheimer's and had diabetes. His health issues made it very difficult to communicate with him, and was but a shadow of the tall, strong, handsome and commanding man he used to be. Our dad died at the age of ninety three, quietly at home in the care of my brother. It was stated that he died of old age, his heart stopped and the coroner's report said dad died of natural causes. So at the age of fifty seven years old I am now an orphan. My parents were caring and committed to being a family and were doing their very best with the knowledge and life experience that they had.

As a child, I was a bit of a tomboy, due to the fact that I thought all the boys got more opportunities and better toys than me. To this day I think I relate better to boys than girls, but others think I relate better to girls. It is my view that girls and boys are no longer in set groups in terms of behaviours, activities and interactions with others. Due to the computer and television era, boys and girls do pretty much the same sort of things and relate to each other and others in accordance with what they see TV stars and singers doing. Hence, we do indeed have a much more cosmopolitan way of interacting which sees more boys sitting down and talking about their feelings and more girls acting out their issues.

I experienced sexual abuse as a child at the hands of someone we referred to as uncle, he was a friend of the family who lived with us. According to common practice of people migrating from Jamaica, he was housed with us for many years until he moved on to live with a partner. This man died when I was about twenty years old. I had confronted him about the abuse, and he said that no one would believe me if I told anyone. My motive for confronting him was to let him know that I would protect younger children in the family if I thought he was abusing them, and indeed when his step-daughter had a girl child, I informed Brent Council children's services, in London, of the abuse I had experienced and the fact that he was not to be trusted. They warned the mother, who was clear that she would protect her child and promptly moved out of his house.

The abuse affected me for many years, but I found counselling from a young age and have used the negative experience to help me support others who have experienced such abuse.

My brothers and father are now aware of the abuse—I told them as an adult. My now deceased brother, Winny, cried when I told him and said he was so sorry that he did not protect me, but nobody really knew what was going on as I was so good at pretending that everything was ok, and the abuser was so smart and skilled at pulling the wool over the family's eyes, today we would call such behaviour, 'grooming'. All my family members thought he was kind, funny and helpful. They adored and admired him, except for my dad, who for some reason never trusted him, but also never really knew just what a danger he was, and so tolerated him.

Unfortunately, my mother died before I had the courage to tell her or my family. My mother was a great woman who would offer support and assistance to all who asked. She had a house full of children but would also look after the children of others when requested—indeed, one woman left a child of a few months' old with Mum and did not return for two whole years. She said the only reason she did return for the child is that she heard that my mum had had more babies. I can hardly remember this boy as I was only about four years old when he left.

As a schoolgirl, I was excellent at sports and ran for the school and played in the netball team. I was quite popular and had several friends. To this day, my two best friends are a girl from my infant school and another I met at the age of twelve. We are very close and spend weekends together and go on holidays together. I enjoyed school even though I was not academic. In fact, I am dyslexic and did not learn to read until the age of nine.

My mother adored me as I was her only girl child. She would take me everywhere with her and would tell everyone what a lovely child I was. It is due to my mother that I have the level of confidence and resilience that I have today.

My mother was an orderly in a local hospital where she worked on the children's ward and fed the children; then she worked on the cancer ward and cared for the dying. On one occasion, my mother brought an elderly white man home and told us that his wife had died of cancer. That man came to our home every Wednesday for some three years for his evening meal. On odd weekends we would also visit him, all of us, including dad.

We sat and ate biscuits and chatted, in this tiny little house where he lived until he died.

My mother had desires of being a school teacher when she left school, and had she stayed in Jamaica, that is what she would have done, but coming to England was not easy and we were quite poor. Mum had to cut up her wedding dress to make shirts for her children, and we could hardly afford to go on school trips if there was a cost involved. However, many other families in the neighbourhood were poor, so it was not as distressing for us as it would be for children nowadays.

Mum died of throat cancer at the age of sixty-two even though she never smoked a day in her life. I was twenty-four years old when she died and missed her dearly, as did my son. At that time, I resided not far from the family home in a council flat. But I was a strong independent young woman who had been working since the age of eighteen in a residential home, so I just got on with my life after grieving for about a year.

My dad had one sister who was also the only girl amongst her six siblings born to her mother, and the only relative of my dad that we grew up with. As my mum and dad worked, they would send me to Birmingham to stay with my dad's sister and her husband for safe keeping. I would go every summer holiday and some Easters. As an adult, I continue to visit my aunt and uncle's home, in Birmingham; it is my safe haven where I go when I want comfort or support, or just a break. My aunt lived to the age of ninety-two and died in a hospice as she could no longer be cared for at home, she could hardly speak and her movement was limited. She was a wonderful woman who used to cook like a dream, knit any and everything and tell the most wonderful stories, but spent her last days trapped in her body unable to express herself. I tried to visit every two months or so and spent the weekend with my uncle who is a great guy that I can say anything to. I knew that he would be attentive and supportive, and we visited my aunt in the hospice. Auntie and Uncle were like second parents to me. In fact, my aunt and my mother were at the birth of my son.

I had my only child at the age of twenty. I really wanted this baby, I really wanted him to be a boy, and thank God he was as I was not sure I could manage the stress of raising a girl, as at that time I thought girls were at more risk of being sexually abused, I now know that this is not true and boys are at risk of abuse too. I spent years asking my son if I had managed to keep him save. PJ is now 37 and tells me that he was indeed safe. I raised my child with the assistance of my family as a single parent. I have remained friends with the child's father, but he had several girlfriends at the time, and I was not prepared to be one of many. To this day we are still good friends, and I have made sure that my son knew his half-brothers and sister; indeed, I am very close to the mothers of my son's siblings and they now visit me from time to time. The daughter that my son's father has refers to me as her step-mum and we are both very close. I told the mothers of the boys—my son's brothers—that one day we will die, so it is best that they, the children know each other and live well together.

My son is a fine young man who I am very proud of. He is doing well in his job and loves it. He has married a lovely young woman, who is a teaching assistant, approximately seven years ago and is well regarded and raising his family in the Christian faith.

I decided that I did not want a stepfather for my son, as I really did not think that I would find someone who I could trust to raise my son the way I wanted him to be raised, hence I kept boyfriends out of the house and only started staying with boyfriends when my son was sixteen years old. I did ask a male friend that I respected and trusted to be a mentor to my son and this man has been great—indeed, to this day, if my son is embarking on a new venture, he will discuss it with this male friend first.

Even though I worked, I ensured that I continued to develop as a professional by taking evening and weekend courses in counselling and other related fields. I have continued to work in the caring profession for over thirty years to date and have worked with all client groups in a number of different settings, such as residential care, social work teams, youth offending teams, probation offices, secure units and hospitals. I have progressed to management level and now am keen on training others in children's mental health and wellbeing, including child protection training. I have managed to combine my personal interest with work, via developing somewhat of an expertise in spiritual abuse and harm to children via faith and culture, in which I offer consultation to professionals, and have developed training packages for community groups and professionals.

I have always been very interested in spirituality and the practice of religion, but I was also quite a feminist and did not like the idea that faith institutions were often male dominated, so it took me quite a while to find an organisation or place of worship that I was happy to join.

In about 2003, I became an interfaith minister, which means I am an ordained minister who can perform weddings, funerals and baby blessings for any one of any denomination or faith as long as they believe in one God, and I have done a few baby blessings and weddings and one funeral to date.

As a single woman, I was really quite happy with my life, although it could get lonely at times, as I lived alone. But I have now achieved most of what I have wanted to in life, including finding a man, that could accept me as a head strong, determined intelligent woman, who is quite complex and sensitive, my husband is as strong, intelligent, complexed and as sensitive as I am. In the future, would like to write a few books, travel a bit more and continue to offer training so that others know how to keep children safe and enable them to become well-functioning adults.

The above synopsis of who I am is just a flavour of all that I have become and a quick look at the foundation from which I came. I shall expand on some aspects of the above-mentioned areas as the book unfolds.

My father Winchester Murray, mother Bernice Eugenie Murray -nee Campbell and my two older brothers, who arrived with my parents from Jamaica in the fifties.

My brother Clement who made the trip from Jamaica to England to be Master if Ceremony at my wedding in 2017

Aunt May and Uncle Dave's wedding in Birmingham, England, July 1961

My mother and I when I was two or three years old, in 1962 or 1963

# Chapter 1

## You Will Grow More Beautiful

I was thirteen years old, or thereabouts, and the neighbours were going to have a big party to which my mum and dad and all the children were invited—yes, all six children. So Mum took me shopping and bought me this cool trouser suit. My hair was taken out of the neat school-suitable plaits and I was allowed to wear it out in an Afro style. My hair was quite thin and wispy, so a lot of patting and grooming was required to get the rounded full Afro look. I had some slick sandals with a little heal on them. The trouser suit was an all-in-one fitted outfit that flared at the bottom. I felt really good and very well dressed. I was such a skinny little thing and had started wearing a bra about a year earlier. I sneaked a little of my mother's green eye shadow and put it on, but she wouldn't let me have any lipstick, so I had to make do with Vaseline.

I felt so excited about going to the party, and all the other neighbours were going to be there.

Dad, of course, in his usual fashion, decided he would not be attending the party, as he preferred to stay home and smoke his pipe. My mum and brothers were taking so long to get ready it was frustrating. I looked out the window and saw lots of people going into the house next door. There were men and women about my parents' age, and some had their children with them. This was an adult party so we felt really privileged to be invited. "Come on, what is taking you lot so long?" I shouted from the bottom of the stairs. My mum shouted back, "If you are ready, you can go before us if you want to." This was music to my ears but not surprising, as we knew the neighbours well and I had been inside their house several times before. But this time it was different, lots of people would be there, especially some of my friends from down the road. I grabbed my little beige clutch bag and off I went.

It did not take me very long to meet up with some of the girls from down the road and the two sisters, Pauline and Norma, who lived next door. I darted into each room to see who was there, saying good evening politely to all the 'big people' who I passed as I was doing so.

The young people all gathered in a little room upstairs and there was loud laughter and lots of fizzy drinks. The party was getting quite full now and there were people all over the house, moving tentatively past each other up and down the stairs. I was on the stairs when a not-too-older man spoke to me. He was a strong good-looking man, dressed in a patterned white and blue shirt. He was not old enough to be my father, but could have been the age of an older cousin. I had never seen him before and as I squeezed past people to get down the stairs on the left-hand side, he was coming up on the right. We met in the middle. He stopped suddenly, so I looked at him because he had interrupted the flow of skilled but tight movement on the stairs. As I came closer to the downstairs landing, I could hear the calypso music from the living room below and the muffled voices of people cheering, chatting and greeting each other. I said, "Excuse me" to the man in the blue-and-white shirt, but he stood there looking at me and then said, in a sure and pondering tone, "The older you get, the more beautiful you'll be." I didn't know how to respond to this, so I smiled and squeezed pass him. The words lingered in my mind as I did not know what he meant. Was this a compliment or was it an insult? Was he just a dirty old man who liked to make passes at children, or was he right that I would become more beautiful with age? The man in the blue-and-white shirt later asked me to keep an eye on his two-year-old son, at which point I decided that he only said I would become beautiful as he wanted me to babysit his kid upstairs while he partied downstairs.

I have spent many years pondering the words of that man who spoke to me on the stairs. I wondered what the words 'to become more beautiful' really meant. Was he possibly referring to an inner beauty or just physical facial looks? Could a person really become more beautiful than they were originally? What this man taught me on a very practical level is that no matter what you are now, there is a possibility that you could be something different tomorrow. It is my view that beauty shines from within and that it indeed grows or fails to grow.

As I have grasped the knowledge that I am about to share with you throughout the pages of this book, I have discovered that beauty manifests on many different levels and that the ability to recognise it even in its infancy is the key to allowing beauty and all things wonderful to be enhanced in your life.

If you are one of those people who likes to read the conclusion first, then do that. But whatever you do, be ready to learn, grow and change.

Whenever we pick up a book, we hope to find something that is meaningful and useful to us. In a strange way, we are often seeking something new, but it must hold something known to us in order for us to identify with it and grow and expand from it. This book will surely do that, but only for those of you who are prepared to look beyond your usual parameters of realistic expectations. I want you to take this opportunity and step out of your comfort zone, that place where all is familiar to you and easily accepted, maybe into a place of deeper enquiry and new discovery.

I know that I will be sharing something so deeply profound and magnificent with you that it will impact on your thinking and hopefully influence your relationship with others, but more importantly, this information may cause you to consider the relationship you have with yourself. We are going to explore the dynamics of spirituality and the truth about human inner power, and this will enable you to reframe every aspect of your life experiences thus far, so that they work in a more constructive way for you in the future. I intend to stimulate your mind, emotions and understanding in a way that most spiritual and empowerment books have not done before. You see, the content of this book is not about how you might understand it on an intellectual level but more about how you experience it on a knowing and enquiring level.

The spirit of the Most High or otherwise known as the universal force, is an amazing thing and if you begin to allow yourself to open up to the spiritual energy of the Most High, the universal force or the higher self—depending on how you identify with the power that works with and through you—it has an uncanny way of bringing experiences into your life that align you with spirit and enable you to learn and know more about it to a degree where you can benefit from every move that you make in life.

I have heard associates and friends say, "Oh you must read that book, it's so powerful it will change your life." Let me tell you up front, here and for real, only you have the power to change your life. The written word can encourage you to perceive things differently or even help you to appreciate a situation that had not been easy for you to make sense of before. Books are wonderful things that can have an influence on your life. In reality, however, books are a collection of words on pages; it's what you do with the comprehension and experience of those words that may change your life. It's like the tongue, it can deliver great words of comfort and healing and yet again the tongue can be as sharp as a sword edge and totally wounding, depending whose mouth it is in and what they wish to express.

When the Bible talks of 'man' having free will, this statement is so far reaching and deep in meaning that I sometimes find the responsibility of the truth behind this completely overwhelming. I shall elaborate more on this topic later. But in brief, you *are* all that there is, and you have *access* to all that there is, with the choice to *limit* all that there is. What is she talking about? I can imagine you might say. Well, by the time you complete this book, you will have a greater understanding of what I mean by you being all that there is an infinitely connected to everything else, and you will be inspired to find out more.

I am so excited. I cannot wait to share some of my experiences and the spiritual understanding of them with you. My life has transformed in ways that I could never have imagined and I will endeavour to explain. And as I share it with you, I am still trying to digest aspects of it myself. You see, the things I am going to tell you about have enhanced my very being and given me so much material, emotional and spiritual wealth, I sometimes can't believe it is true, even though I was the one who experienced it. I promise you every word written in this book is the absolute truth. The interpretation of my experiences is, of course, my own and you may read my account of events and come to a totally different conclusion. That is fine, for it is in the dialogue and the ability to debate that we have the opportunity to rethink our views and possibly change our behaviours for the greater good of ourselves and others. I perceive myself as a fun-loving, logical-thinking woman. I am educated to master's degree level, which simply means some others better educated than myself agree that I know a little something about training staff in social work and managing those in social work. I am down to earth and practical, a sensible rational person—well, most of the time.

I come from a humble, poor background influenced by my Jamaican parents, who, like many others, thought that education was the best way forward and that every girl should learn how to keep a good house, cook well and always be clean and tidy. I only passed one exam in school and that was home economics, commonly known as cookery class. As previously stated, when I was a small child, I was the victim of sexual abuse, I was however, not sexually abused by my father, mother or any of my five brothers whom I grew up with, nor my two other brothers who grew up in Jamaica apart from us. As agreed by my brothers, I share this information with you so that you know that it was not them that hurt me and caused my childhood to be something I could not wait to grow out of, in the hope that adulthood would be a better experience. Indeed, although not perfect, adulthood is proving to be a better experience than childhood, for at long last I now have more control of what happens to me.

The sexual abuse had a devastating effect on my childhood and left me very depressed and somewhat trapped in a world where I felt constantly terrified, disgustingly dirty and trusting of no one. On the inside I was forever crying, with a sense of worthlessness that culminated in me attempting to take my life at fifteen years old. Yet my outer character was skilled at pretending to be alright, strong and sociable. I would smile, chat and participate in school activities. Indeed, at the age of fifteen years old, in the year of 1976, I was the fastest 100-metre sprint runner in the British Isles. At the same time in the world championships, held in Montreal, Canada, German Anne Richter, broke the world record coming in at a time of 11.0. Around that time I actually broke that record coming at 11 seconds dead. Unfortunately, when I was growing up, in a household that would be described as relatively poor, we could not afford things like a fridge, or our own home, and running shoes with spikes, were definitely not affordable, hence my career as a potential athlete was never realised. I was skilled at pretending to be absolutely normal, when it felt like everything about me was either crumbling or already dead. However, I truly believe that it is the struggles that I experienced throughout my life that have now enabled me to say that I am sincerely content and happy with most of the time and I experience an inner feeling of security and a deep sense of belonging to something greater than myself. I now feel like I belong, at least to myself, and have a purpose. I can see my part in the world, and I am aware of the influence, positive and occasionally negative, that I have on others. I am aware of my strengths and weaknesses and I have skilfully learnt how to compensate for what I might lack in personal attributes through valuing others and knowing when to ask for help. Yet most importantly, I have the capacity to cope if help is not forthcoming from those I might turn to. Through extreme adversity, I have learnt to develop self-reliance and resilience.

In spite of the fact that I raised a son, who is also dyslexic, as a lone parent, from the age of twenty, and experienced racism and oppression within my community and at work, I managed to develop a successful career in the caring profession with very little support but for the grace of God. I have managed to achieve the normal things in life, and I am able to cover my bills and gain some material and financial stability. I now own two properties in London and Kent, one consisting of seven bedrooms. I am an accomplished public speaker and trainer offering and sharing my knowledge about children's mental health and child protection needs to a wide and varied audience of professional and community groups across the globe. women and men; I also offer my services as a spiritual counsellor. These accomplishments help me to feel like a worthy part of society, doing the same things others do from day to day, and I am still able to hold hope for a better tomorrow.

The greatest thing that I have ever done was to raise my wonderful, well-grounded and spiritual son, Parez-Jade Murray. He is a totally gorgeous young black man, with a strong and honest character, kind and considerate to others, hardworking and succeeding as a sales manager. He is honouring and committed to his lovely wife and a conscientious father to his children. My son was raised to know that he is infinitely connected to a great source, and that that connection makes him important and valuable. He is also very loved and cared for by this invisible powerful source, that some call God, Allah or Jah, and others call the power of the universe or connection with the higher self. I told my son that he was this force and this force was him and that all people, animals and plants are part of this great force. When my son was a young boy, he went to school and shared this philosophy about being infinitely connected to a source greater than all its parts, with his Religious Education teacher during a class lesson. The teacher reprimanded him for being disruptive in class. When PJ told me this, I reminded him that even though the source is available to us all, no matter what our race, gender or beliefs may be, not all of us are ready to receive it and make best use of it. My son is now a devoted Christian and is still aware of the amazing source that he now refers to as Jesus, Son of God, and that he, my son, is indeed still connected to that wonderful source.

When raising a child, it is every parent's fear that they will somehow not be a good enough parent or will fail to guide and protect their child. Well, can you imagine my fear? I hardly had enough money to buy what we needed, and I was struggling with the history of childhood sexual abuse—so much so, that I could hardly play rough and tumble with my child. When it came to protecting my son from abuse, I was OTT, (over the top) almost to the point of smothering the child with protective guidance. Some mothers and fathers who have experienced sexual abuse in childhood are very worried that maybe they will perpetrate the same abusive behaviour on their own children, to such a degree that some choose not to have children. It was never my fear that I would sexually abuse my child. I was very clear that I had no desire to interact with children in a sexual way, but I did fear that I would somehow fail to protect my child from sexual predators, or–that, like my mother I would not be able to read the signs of how abusers get close to families through grooming for preparation of abuse. I feared that I would not be able to see the abuser coming or be able to recognise that I was being conned, so that someone could hurt my child. Hence, in order to protect my child and myself from further abuse, I decided never to trust anyone, so that way they could not get close enough to hurt me or my son.

This took a lot of energy and was extremely hard work. I had to be constantly vigilant and always trying to second guess what the motive or plans of others were who tried to get close to us. I also had to be very independent and do as much as I could for myself so that there was no reason for others to get too close. I was always ready to cease any relationship at any time, if I held the slightest thought that they were not genuine or that they might hurt my son. This meant I did not invest much in people or my relationship with them and was ready to do without them at any time.

You can imagine how this made me into a cold and calculating person and how this left my son with the view that one had to be ready to fend for oneself as very few people could really be trusted. I recall that my son Parez wanted to go on a camping trip with the school summer scheme. The organiser was a man called Marcus Garvey, probably named after the pioneering Jamaican activist of the same name. After intense soul searching, I came to the conclusion that I could not wrap my son up in cotton wool forever and that I had to take some chances and indeed trust someone else with his wellbeing. I agreed that my son could go on this trip. I packed his bag for a week and we got into my little green car and drove down to the school. There we waited outside the school gate on an early Friday evening, where several other parents gathered with excited little children who all had small rucksacks on their backs and were filled with frenzied excitement about going away together to spend time outdoors in tents with open fires and a timetable of rugged fun for a week. I said to the modern Mr Marcus Garvey, camp leader, "I am leaving my son in your care, and no one else, trust me if this child is hurt or distressed in any way, if you fail to protect him from harm, I will be holding you solely responsible and I will kill you and that is not a figure of speech. If you cannot assure me that you will protect him, tell me now so I can take my son home where he will be safe."

Mr Garvey looked at me and I think he knew I was serious. Then he got into his usual parental assurance mode and said, "We do this all the time and your son will be fine." I quickly and firmly responded, "I don't care what you usually do; tell me now that you will make sure that he is safe." Mr Garvey, realising that I was not going to be appeased by his usual parental comfort speech, told me that if I was not happy about the arrangements that were in place, then maybe I should not send my son on this trip. At this point, I looked in the distance and could see Parez with his little bag on his back like all the others. He was full of joyous anticipation and gleefully chatting away to school friends about the pending adventure, and I thought to myself, as much as I would have liked to take my son straight back home at that point, I had indeed made the decision to take a chance on life and let him live a little outside of my over-zealous protection.

I said to Mr Garvey one more time, "Bring him back to me as I have given him to you, or you will never live to go on one of these trips again and I mean it."

They went camping. I waited alongside other parents two weeks later when they returned on the coach outside the school. It was early evening on a dry summer day. Parents gathered and smiled at each other, all hoping that their children had returned safely. Mr Garvey emerged from the mass of children, who had come streaming off the big white coach, holding my son's hand and said, "See? He is absolutely fine and he had a great time, so I am handing him back to you now," poor Marcus Garvey.

My son was full of camping cheer with several stories to tell. I just smiled at Mr Garvey and felt stupid for being so worried and over protective. I thanked him and quickly left the busy playground scene.

Looking at my polite, well-behaved son now and considering the man he has turned out to be, I am so proud and relieved that he is more than fine. Parez is thriving and progressing with dignity, integrity and ambition in abundance. What more could any mother ask?

At PJs and his beautiful wife V, had a wonderful tropical-themed wedding, I felt quite embarrassed at the number of compliments I was given for raising such a fine young man. The mother of the bride has said to me, "I wish we could clone your son—I would like the exact version of such a man, to marry my younger daughter." Well, I was speechless and happy that I had done a good job. The credit is not all mine, however. While raising my child, we were given some difficult experiences and trials which I am sure have shaped my son's thinking. Credit also needs to be given to Parez (PJ) because as a child he had the ability to grasp the concept that he is far greater and more powerful because he is connected and has access to the power of a higher source.

When I consider the amount of adversity that I had experienced ever since my birth and the fact that I can now hold my head high and say life is truly worth living and is so very rewarding, I want to tell you about how I have come to be where I am today.

Yes! It is true I have always been extremely stubborn and determined to do things my own way—so much so that my mother used to say, "Your stubbornness will be the death of you." Hence in true stubborn style, I decided it would be the making and success of me. I became very focused on what I wanted to achieve. I worked extremely hard at achieving my goals and refused to give up, unless there was really no other option left to try. This habit of being really driven and determined has served me well for the best part, but, on occasion, I have been known to take it to the extreme, for example when driving somewhere, if I find that I have gone the wrong way and need to turn back, my stubborn streak tells me that if I just keep going I will surely find a way round and back to my destination without turning back. This has caused me to drive many miles out of my way, and finally I have had to succumb to the fact that sometimes the only way to go forward is indeed to turn back at least for a while. I have now learnt to curb my stubbornness and to accept that sometimes I might get it wrong. I have learnt to be more flexible and accepting of others' choices or suggestions as to how things can be achieved. I have an appreciation that it is ok to change one's mind and do something different.

All these lessons in life are very important and it is true that if you want to succeed or achieve something, the rules of applying yourself diligently are crucial. So, the application of discipline, hard work and ambition with planned goals has allowed me to accomplish a great deal. However, without the unconditional love and support from an amazing source, connected to me but not of me, I would never have been able to realise the level of so much happiness and contentment that I am able to experience at this stage in my life. I would never have realised the material things that are now in my possession or travelled so extensively and met such amazing people all over the world. In order to explore the power of spirit, there are things that I am going to tell you about that I could not possibly have achieved by myself. Without the help of spirit, the great source, the universal force, the Most High, my life would be a totally different story.

We are living in a time of immense confrontation; in society, nowadays, we face the challenge of unexpected aggression on many levels. Some experience this in their homes as domestic violence, and others have angry and frustrated parents who find it hard to express happiness and peace towards them or others. Even in our places of work, we sometimes find we are faced with unnecessary competition, bullying and rejection.

Many are facing levels of poverty that have not been experienced in the last fifty years or more. We all face the threat of unprovoked violence—in the streets, pubs and clubs, and even on holiday.

We live in a society where giving has become a commercial event, often only done for personal gain or tax relief. People are feeling isolated and alone as our world has entered the technical digital age of solitude with machines for company, whether they take the form of an iPad, computer, mobile phone or digital television. Children and young people living in western society are experiencing bereavement and loss on a scale that is hardly believable through the impact of knife crime, gang violence, drug related deaths, HIV/Aids and cancer—as well as illnesses in general. Last, but not least, divorce and separations are tearing families apart, leaving children feeling lost and confused. This leaves us with a society that is filled with fear of others and often of self too, as well as a sense of loss of love. As we struggle with all these issues, the world suffers too. The natural world is also suffering, our climate is changing in a way that threatens the existence of our plants, animals and the planet.

So, what is really happening in our world and what is it all about? How should we address the situation? I think it is time we acknowledged that there is a void in our lives and experiences, and that this void disturbs the equilibrium of the natural order of things. We have lost a sense of balance; hence our political leaders suggest extreme methods that only serve to curtail our free will, criminalise our very desperate young people, and limit our future entrepreneurs by stifling free expression and quality of life—not to mention lack of appropriate comfortable, affordable living spaces for all.

*"Many of us would like the world to change, but we don't want to endure the trouble of helping make that happen. It's easier to dream of better leaders who give charismatic speeches about community or civil rights, decreases or increases in military and police protection, improvements in the economy and the betterment of humankind..."* (Mindell A. Chapter 1, p.18)

So, as you can see, we face a major problem, for self and others. Some are taking steps within the political arena to address the issues they can, others are attempting to reach out to members of our community to offer them guidance with addressing the daily problems that they face. Some are doing the best they can to keep themselves safe and their heads above water—and by so doing, not adding to the many difficulties that society has to face. I suggest, however, that their efforts only serve to address the scars of the problem rather than the source of the pain.

It is now time that we cut back the weeds of our worldly distress and go to the root of the problem, the void between our true selves and the universal balance. It is my view that our efforts will be in vain if we fail to reconnect with our inner strengths and spiritual powers, which will allow us to realign with the spiritual forces and reinstate our collective and worldly energetic balance.

My path in life continues to be an interesting and complex experience, culminating in my very true sense of hope and trust that we can find our way to a better place of being for all, on many different levels.

Within these pages I will make reference to my experience of having experienced sexual abuse as a small baby and young child, at the hands of a family friend, whom my parents embraced and trusted. I am now fifty-eight years old and somehow that experience still manages to impact on my life, but due to the spiritual empowerment that I have cultivated, the impact is often in being of service to other survivors both male and female and young and old, from many different walks of life. The level of poverty that I experienced in childhood also shaped my future. I can now say that I have the ability to manifest abundance, and money in particular, which has changed my expectation and vision of who can and can't have wealth. By the spiritual tools that I have practised and mastered, I am able to change my life experiences for the better on so many different levels in terms of happiness, fulfilling one's dreams and knowing so much more about life. I really want to share that knowledge with you, as I know that it is possible for all to experience a different level of being, beyond current expectations and that healing from the worse life experience is very possible.

We have an inner power that we are failing to make best use of, and, in not using this power, we are creating a void between us and the universal energy flow, which ultimately creates a society of desperation, fear and greed. The information you are about to be party to is my attempt to equalise the imbalance of universal law and inner spiritual power. May your journey be fulfilling, abundant and prosperous!

But my reason for writing this book has nothing to do with vanity or a need to boast of how far I have got on my personal spiritual journey. Personal spiritual journey? Now there's a strange concept or is it! My desire in writing these thoughts and experiences of connecting with spirit is more to do with a burning desire to express and share something that I have sincerely come to know—about what could and does happen, when we allow the God force within ourselves to manifest. I am aware that when we appreciate how spirit works with us and amongst us, everything and everybody in our lives is transformed, for the better including us.

By the very fact that you have read these few lines and hopefully have opened your mind up to the possibility that there might be more to learn about spirit, I know that spirit will draw closer to you, so already positive change may well be happening in your life. Let us now start to look at how to recognise and value it, so that we can use it constructively for ourselves and others. THIS IS YOUR GOD-GIVEN RIGHT.

Thank you for allowing me through these pages to be part of your spiritual journey to self.

This little book is just a short introduction to the spiritual energy that is available to empower your life. The fact that you opened this book is an expression of your inner knowing, of the intention of enhancing your life, wellbeing and abundance. In so doing, you have evidenced appropriate action towards spiritual growth. Well done.

The following brief chapters will take you through an understanding of the innate power within you and reveal ways of developing connection with the higher source, which has always been available to you. It's a bit like looking for your glasses when, all the time, they have been right there on your face. When you realise this, knowing how they got there does not matter anymore. It's just the way it is and you can see clearly now.

This book was written out of spiritual inspiration. The night I started, I could hardly stop writing and I could not sleep. I was so filled with excitement at the very idea of sharing these thoughts with you and others. Yes, it's fine to pass this book onto others, once you have got what you wanted to receive from it. And when that time comes, you will know. Or maybe you will be generous enough to get that person whom you would like to share this experience with, a copy of their very own, in the spirit of giving and receiving, about which we will say more later.

Who is this *we*? You might wonder. Well, I am not so vain, self-centred or so self-righteous as to presume that these words and wisdom flow only from me. What I am about to share with you, has been known to our ancestors, grandparents and innocent children from time before time. As the spirit within us holds the key to this knowledge, I have been blessed with the task, ability and duty to summarise this information in a fashion that makes it possible for you to digest easily. But be aware, as you consume this information, that you must chew slowly and diligently, as what you are about to absorb is very, very powerful indeed and worthy of your full attention and discerning mind.

You are in charge of what you do with the information that you receive. More importantly, only you can decide how and whether you allow the contents of this book to impact on your life. Note I did not say *influence* your life, because this is not about trying to influence you. As you will recall, we are looking for something you already have and are possibly already making some use of in your daily life. However, once you know you have got it and recognise it for all that it is, you will have a better opportunity of working with it more effectively to the enhancement of your life and the lives of others. So, in order for you to see more clearly, let's start looking.

In order to make effective use of the universal laws we must appreciate that we are infinitely connected to everything and everyone and most importantly we are aware that our body mind and soul, is our part of the kingdom which is a small part of a greater kingdom that we call life. Life is the living and being within the world and within ourselves.

A friend and I were invited by a neighbour to Sunday dinner. We knew that the food would be just fine as she was a cook at the local Caribbean elderly day centre. On arrival she announced that she was not hungry, but suggested *we* should get stuck in. My friend and I looked at each other and then said to her, "No, girl, if you are not eating neither are we." It's not that we did not trust her or her cooking, but we did not feel comfortable eating whilst she stood by and watched, and maybe there was a bit of us that didn't totally trust her. She got a small side plate and served herself a tiny portion of everything—at which point we felt better, and all enjoyed the meal. It was important for my neighbour to honour herself first by including herself in the partaking of the food, in order to allow us, her guests, to feel honoured by her.

In the same way, if we are to honour the spiritual energy within us, we not only need to know that we are the kingdom; we need to honour that kingdom first. This is a basic universal law, which will be explained in the next few sentences. If spirit is to dwell where we are, we need to be home sometime. Let me put it this way. Imagine your body, mind and soul is this vast space that houses your character, personality, emotions, pains, pleasures, ethics and thoughts. Within this space there is a seat available for the spirit to dwell and if spirit dwelled there, character would be acknowledged as strong and worthy, personality would be seen as charming and acceptable, emotion would feel calm and balanced, pain and pleasure would find harmony amongst each other, ethics would find spirit to be a great sounding board and wise adviser, and thought would have the power to express and create all that was desired. However, on spirit's arrival, it finds all the other seats empty. Where is emotion, pain, ethics and thought? Where have they all gone? Spirit sits and waits for them to return. For a fleeting moment pain appears and thought and emotion keep popping in and out, as do all the others. Spirit sits and waits. Finally, spirit feels so cut off and separate from the rest who are housed in the mind, soul and body, that it just sits there dormant, not even noticing any more who pops in and out, or whether the return is fleeting or enduring.

If we are too busy finding ways to numb our feelings and pains, too busy seeking after the next bout of pleasure, denying our emotions and values, never considering who we are, what we believe or what we stand for; if we are too wrapped up in other people's business, or too busy fearing things which we have no control over and generally fire-fighting, then what room in our lives is there for spirit? Yet without spirit we have no option but to live in a disjointed way, separate from ourselves, never knowing what we are really feeling or what the most recent experience is trying to teach us. It is so important that we acknowledge that we have a spirit within us that requires us to know that it is there and has a purpose in our lives. Through spirit every aspect of us is fuelled with all the life force energy that we need. Spirit is the conductor that connects all our parts and life experiences to the body and the other elements on the planet, including the Most High, and all it requires is our awareness of its existence. Once we are consciously aware of spirit then we are infinitely connected to the laws of the universe that govern our experiences and align us with our greater good.

The term universal law refers to the natural order and sequence of things, for example life and death, cause and effect, etc. There are many universal laws which play a part in our lives, whether we are aware of them or not. My mother, God rest her soul, had a wonderful saying: *Who can't hear, must feel.* Now as a child, I thought she meant, if you don't listen to what I am saying to you, you are 'gonna' feel it with a smack. I soon grew to realise that what Mum really meant was, if you don't listen to the lessons of life, life will teach them to you the hard way. This is something I am sure we can all identify with. But I am not talking about ignoring good advice given to you by others. I am talking about ignoring good advice given to you from within you. Yes, that gut feeling that we have and sometimes ignore. The inner voice that we choose not to hear. You see, deep within us, we are aware of the spiritual laws, which I think are infinitely connected to the universal laws. However, due to upbringing, peer pressure and societal rules, we often get very confused as to what we really think, or what we think the world might approve of. In honouring ourselves, we would take time to work out just what our views are, whether they are in agreement with the rest of society, and whether we care if they are or are not anyway. There are no right or wrong answers, but getting to know and value who you are and what you really stand for, think and believe, gives you an opportunity to stick with what you have discovered about yourself, or change it if you would prefer to do so, based on the new-found knowledge and insight of self. But before you can even think about changing, you must know what it is or what aspects of yourself, you would or might like to change or adjust.

In honouring ourselves we learn to accept ourselves and love the parts of us that others might find challenging. Even if the rest of the world does not think that we are great, it is so important that we do. Why? Because it is only in our lives and our being, that our part of spirit can dwell comfortably and help us live a more content and fulfilled life. No one else can do this for you, which means you are the most important person to yourself.

Remember our mind, body and soul is the kingdom in which the spirit resides and works through us to bring about all that we need in life, and if we are appropriately in tune, we can also gain some of our wants and desires. We therefore need to value ourselves through a range of nourishing experiences. We nourish our mind through relaxation and contemplation, we nourish our emotions through sweet memories and comforting thoughts, we nourish our bodies through healthy food and a good variety of exercise and rest. We nourish our soul through feeding the spirit. So how do you feed the spirit? Imagine being in love with someone who is just as much in love with you. Some other person has chosen to hold you in high regard, that person has chosen to make you special, to adore you, think about you and consider what would please you. Because that other person expresses this feeling of love towards you and you have chosen to accept and reciprocate, an amazing thing happens, feelings well up inside you. All of a sudden you feel powerful, happy, far more confident and content. You have an urge to let the whole world know how great you feel, and some even go as far as to say, "I feel like I am on cloud nine, out of this world." Others say, "I feel so great, it's almost like I can do or be anything I want to." Oh yes, it's a marvellous feeling, being in love, and everything about you shines.

Now imagine that spirit is 'inloveness' turned inward. There is no other, no outside person. Yet all of a sudden, spirit sees you and you see spirit. Within that moment, you fall in love with all parts of yourself. You have an acceptance of your body, no matter how it looks, you value the knowledge you have received to date and you have a great respect for who you are. You have a desire to eat better and to look after yourself; you want to be fit and healthy. You desire to intake all that will nourish your spirit. The truth of the matter is that spirit cannot be fed or nourished unless we are nourishing ourselves in every possible way. You see, spirit is a divine reflection of you. Spirit lights up and becomes motivated once you realise that it is there. Spirit is willing and able to support you, but only in as much as you expect it to.

This is deep, so listen carefully. Spirit does not need you, you need it! As spirit is our silent yet relevant driving force, in truth you and spirit are inseparable. However, that does not stop you from pretending it does not exist and that spirit is not there. You know, the way we sometimes behave when we have family that we cannot abide, we simply avoid them and pretend that they don't exist and if we can, we move far away from them. But deep in our hearts we know they will always be family and indeed we share spiritual energy with them, which is how and why they arouse such strong feelings within us. Family is also what allows us to feel whole when stressors in life cause us to withdraw into ourselves and hide from the world. Family reminds us that we belong, and in connecting to family we enhance our sense of spiritual completeness.

From the moment of inception, yes long before you even were born, when you and spirit could not be defined as anything but whole, spirit agreed to always be of service to you and to always sustain you, in line with the laws of the universe. Hence, you breath, live, grow and die, but spirit never dies. Spirit remains a part of you, whatever form your mind, body and soul may take. Most importantly, spirit is so powerful, tolerant, understanding and patient that spirit just waits quietly for you to remember that it is there, ready and able to support and assist you. Once this realisation is apparent, then spirit reflects in your life, and to the rest of the world, all that you are and more. Once you acknowledge the presence of spirit, all the aspects of yourself are able to pull together and bring into being your every need. Spirit is like the mirror to your soul, that part of you that is enduring, creative, resourceful and powerful. In order to thrive, we need to remember who we are. You know what it is like when you pass a mirror and catch an image of yourself and think, oh my God is that me? Then you get a glimpse of how the world might see you, but more importantly you remember how you perceive yourself.

Once the spirit, mind, soul and body are able to embrace themselves, wholeness is resumed and you are ready to reach out and create, achieve and experience, more than you could ever imagine. To get to this stage in our spiritual growth, however, there are other matters we need to consider and master. Here is where it gets really interesting. You will recall that I said that spirit will only help you in so much as you expect it to or trust it to. So, what else do we need to know in order to build our spiritual muscles? Keep listening my friend, keep hearing what is being said, and some more will be revealed, but not all. Why? Because all of the answers are with you and not with me. This is true for each of us. Yes, every single one of us.

There are times in our lives when we find it extremely difficult to honour ourselves, such as in those moments, months or even years, when we feel as though we are not giving life our best or maybe when we feel that we lack the opportunity to really express who we are. In situations such as loneliness, lack of funds, stuck in a dead-end job that does not even cover the bills, desperately loving someone who is not keen on expressing that love back to us, or maybe failing at a lifelong ambition. All these situations can leave us feeling emotionally and energetically drained, with little desire to think positively. It is at this very moment, that deep within us we have the capacity to be most creative and powerful. If we can only get past the crap on the surface of our being, then we can find the gem that desperately wants to shine from deep within us. When we are feeling at our lowest point, then the reservoir of potent energy is stimulated. But at these very difficult times of trials and tribulations, we often end up using this most internal resourceful energy just to keep going from day to day.

Herein lies the ultimate challenge that we may have to face—to try and utilise some of our survival energy to create positive things in our lives. We may not have the ability to convince the bank manager to give us that desperately needed overdraft, and no matter how sweet the perfume or that special Sunday dinner, that adored lover is not coming back. All these things are outside of our immediate control. Hence, we often end up fretting, wishing and hoping for them, to no avail, when we could be doing something far more constructive and something that is within the realm of our power. We could take at least one hour out of our distressing time, each day, to find time and space for ourselves and make a conscious effort to let go of the worries, just for that hour. Then spend the time visualising, imagining, daydreaming or just thinking of a situation that we would like in our lives. And in that hour, make this fantasy enjoyable. See the situation as if it is happening right now. Take a few moments to relax and try this simple exercise that follows.

Imagine the feeling of joy and happiness in any particular situation where you are content and happy, think of a past situation where you felt this or create a fantasy situation where you are so happy and satisfied. Then pretend that people are talking about how wonderful, content and happy you are. Paint the picture in your mind, think of the smells, the colours and sounds that would be around you in your given and chosen desired situation. Make yourself smile about it and relish in this beautiful fantasy for a while. This is not an easy task, as the troubled mind will keep harping back to the worries that seem like the only reality in this space of frustration, fear and gloom. If it helps, use the aid of music to lift your spirits, put on clothes that make you feel good. Turn the heating up or wrap up in a cosy blanket, but whatever you do, get warm and comfortable so that you find it easy to relax, just for this hour. When you have finished creating that amazing story in your head, then see that wonderful situation wrapped in something that feels safe and secure to you. Something like bubble wrap, cotton wool, or strong firm muscles, whatever feels safe to you. Then see the wonderful fantasy coated all over with love that is your image of love, whatever that might look like.

Once the scene is set in your mind's eye, then imagine your awesome situation that gave you such bliss, sinking from your head, down your spine and finding its way deep within your heart. Guess what it might feel like to have that wonderful situation filling your heart—is it warm, does it glow, is it soothing or exciting? Now imagine that your wonderful situation is deliciously edible with all that joy and happiness still contained within it. Feel this sensation in your stomach, nourishing and satisfying, removing any sense of hunger or anxiety. Take a moment to enjoy this feeling of being filled with your desire. Next imagine your great and pleasurable situation as oxygen running through your veins, all over your body, up your arms and down your fingers, from head to toe. Is the pleasurable situation coursing through your veins or is it moving in a cool gentle fashion, like a slow-motion flowing that mingles with your blood in perfect harmony? What does this situation feel like now in your veins? Does it tingle? Is there numbness? Does it tickle your skin? Finally, see your loving exciting, successful situation as air-like energy, still filled with the pleasure and joy originally perceived. Feel this sensation of your situation now light and free, seeping out of your tiny pores and every orifice of your body, filling the room with a sparkly glow. What colour is this situational energy now? Does it have a sweet smell or is it a strong smell? Is the air around you warmer or cooler? Take three deep breaths and inhale this energy back into your lungs. Fill your chest with this marvellous situation, take it all in, it is yours, created and developed right where you are. As you breathe out, know that this magnificent powerful attainable situation, permeates every aspect of your being. Know that your chosen situation is now alive and expanding. But more importantly, you have planted precious seeds that must manifest in your life and reality, sooner or later. How much sooner or later is totally up to you and will depend on how long you allow worry and fear to dominate your thoughts and energy.

Having done this exercise you may feel exhilarated, calm or even weak. Whatever you feel is fine. Your mind, body and spirit know what is best for you to feel at this time and will be guiding you. If this exercise is done well, your anxieties, fretting and worries will be far from your mind as there will be no room for them anymore, at least for a while.

Once the exercise of positive situational saturation is complete, please allow yourself time to absorb the impact and just let your thoughts and feelings be. It would be powerfully reinforcing, if you were to choose to take pen and paper or computer and write down what your situation is and how you are left feeling about the experience. If writing is not your thing, then draw your situation and some representation of your afterthoughts and feelings. It would be most useful to share your experience with someone who you respect and who will listen to you with honour and good wishes for you. If, like many of us, you do not have someone in your life that will hear your words, respect them and support you in believing the possibility of them, take my humble advice: do not tell a living soul. It is better to keep it to yourself than have others rubbish your hard work and trample all over the seeds you took such time and energy to plant.

Furthermore, having done such beautiful positive work, possibly at a time when life is testing you, you really do not require the negative energy of others who may fear change in you or themselves. What you could do is to share your thoughts with the memory of a loved one who has passed, or who is no longer in your life. Just imagine you are sitting with them and talk to them, tell them how wonderful your situational idea is and how great you feel about it. As well as the prospects of it, mention how keen you are to see the manifestation of this magnificent creational dream. Whatever you do, please allow yourself to be acknowledged and heard in any way you can. By doing this, spirit will know that you mean it. This is like feeding spiritual super grow to your situational positive seeds that you recently planted.

Speaking or evidencing your truth about your new-found awesome situation will propel it into action and furnish it with contours and added extras that you couldn't possibly imagine. I am tempted to say: 'wait and see', but you would be ill-advised. It is crucial at this point that you do not wait, but start living your situation here and now, make plans and take even the smallest action towards it. Either the desired affect will manifest in your life, or something even greater will come to be. Honouring yourself for just an hour each day will keep so many negative experiences and situations out of your life and far away from you. Your new actions of positivity and future aims will create better health, happiness and prosperity in your life and you will come to see that indeed you are growing more beautiful.

# Chapter 2

## Life-changing Experiences

In life we come across situations that impact on us forever. Some of these experiences are pleasurable but more often than not they are shocking and distressing. What is always true is that we will never know which experiences will impact on our lives in a way that will adjust the way we relate to ourselves and others in dramatic and revealing ways. The other known truth is that some of us will react to things that others will hardly even notice. A woman could have a child or lose a baby and this will change her outlook on life forever, whereas others will have babies and miscarriages and this will hardly change anything for them in the future. It is also true that some of us will have to endure childhood abuse which may scar us for life whereas others will endure childhood abuse and this may be the catalyst that sets us on a path of resilience and greater strength in spite of the pain and trauma. We are all very different and how we react to situations has a great deal to do with our early attachments to those who raised us, or the lack of attachments to those who raised us. We are also influenced by our sense of hope and self-worth and the hope and worthiness giving to us by others. All these matters will be explored later on.

I would like to share a few of the experiences that have shaped my life and offer an analysis as to how they have impacted on my life, so that you can gain some insight into how your experiences might have impacted on your life or not, depending of whatever the case might be for you.

As previously stated, my beginnings were somewhat shaky and at times scary for me and indeed for my mother. I was born in July some three weeks after my mother's sister, Aunt Daisy, had died. Aunt Daisy had told my mother that this time she would have a girl child, after having four boys and probably two miscarriages. I am not sure where in her childbearing years my mother went through the losses of her pregnancies, but she experienced a stillbirth as well as the miscarriages and only ever had one girl, me. I was born two minutes to midnight on a Friday evening in a small hospital in West Kensington, London, and true to form in my quest to always be different, I was born feet first. Nowadays my mother would have been given a Caesarean birth but back in the day women were allowed to have breach babies or those born feet first. I feel blessed that I came into this world in a fashion that was unusual and somewhat risky. It may have been my very first lesson in surviving adversities, and who knows what level of resistance and resilience this experience might have equipped me with, having survived such an ordeal. I walked at seven months old, and I am told that I had the skinniest little legs and was such a fragile small child—I think, even at that tender age, I was trying to escape from what I somehow knew would follow. I was what my mother would describe as a sickly little child, always suffering with colds and other minor ailments. At one point my mother had to suck the cold from my nose with her mouth, God bless her. I could never do that for my own child and when the moment arrived, and my son's nostrils were very blocked up and he had difficulty breathing, I had to call on my brother Winston to do this, as the thought of it made me feel physically sick.

My mother totally cherished me and I believe this was my saving grace—she so desperately wanted a daughter and I was truly precious to her. Mum taught me everything she thought I should know and more. She was extremely protective and attentive to my needs and desires, but this did not save me from a childhood of absolute pain, distress and constant despair, but might have given me the emotional and psychological cushion that I needed to survive such an ordeal. Mum was protective and loving. However, a person she deemed to be a close relative took advantage of her kind nature and proceeded to deceive her so that he could take advantage of my innocent childhood body. The abusive relative tricked us all in the family by pretending to be kind and helpful when his real motive was to be sexually abusive to a small child. He succeeded in doing that, but he never succeeded at stealing my soul even though he nearly broke my spirit. Do I forgive him? Sometimes—but most of the time I am just pleased that I survived. What I have learnt to do is to no longer blame my mother and I now perceive her as an added victim of the abuse.

I am the woman that I am today because of all that I experienced in childhood and survived. Therein lies the blessing.

I want to tell you about an amazing experience that I had as an adult which is in a strange way connected to the ordeals of childhood pain. I had the opportunity to work in New Zealand for a year as a consultant to a youth offender secure facility. While there, my contract came to an end and I had a few months' break. A colleague of mine noticed an ad in the local social work paper that talked of the need for social workers on an exotic island. I was waiting for my contract to be renewed, as promised by the manager, so was not really looking for more work, but was intrigued. I rang the number and enquired about the post, stating that I was highly skilled and that I did not have time for anything that was not genuine and professional social work, even going as far as saying on the phone that I did not wish them to waste my time. I was invited to an interview.

I was seen by two people from New Zealand, a man and a woman, who told me that the post was in the Pitcairn Islands and that it was for three months. They proceeded to ask me how I would feel about using a pit toilet. Otherwise known as a long drop, this is a whole dug into the ground, usually six feet deep, for use as a toilet when there are no internal toilets available in the property. They told me that I would not be able to leave Pitcairn island until the three months was up, because the ship only came to the island every three months. The shocking information was that if I died they would bury me on the island as they did not have facilities to keep bodies for more than twelve hours.

Well, this sounded like a real adventure, in a hot tropical island very far from home and normality. Being crazy and totally fascinated by the opportunity of doing something so different and somewhat risky, I wanted to say yes on the spot. WHY? I heard more. They had no television or radio, but they did have computers. There were no mobile phones or other phones, only a satellite phone that did not work so well. The island consisted of forty-seven people, six of the men had recently been convicted of sex offences against several women and historical abuse against children.

My role would be to monitor and protect the six children left on the island and befriend and support all of the adults, including the offending men who were in the process of appealing the convictions and awaiting sentencing if they lost that appeal. It was quite a challenge. I was very ready for it.

Pitcairn Islands is in the South Pacific Ocean, it is two by one miles and cut off from all civilisation, except for satellite phones and the internet. I learnt that the inhabitants of the island were direct descendants of those depicted in the film *Mutiny on the Bounty*, the story of Captain Bligh and Christian. Well, after succeeding at the interview and accepting the three-month post, I set out on a long journey to get there. Having travelled for three days on plane and boat, I arrived at Pitcairn Islands with the replacement doctor and two police officers from Scotland. On our arrival we had to go on a speed boat to get near to the island. We then went on a long boat that the members of the island had built, as the ship could not get near to the rocky coast, due to the weather and the treacherous conditions on the two by one mile island.

We were met by a few rugged-looking men who informed us that we had to wait for the waves to rise, and at that point we had to take their hand and trust to God that they could heave us onto the long boat that would take us to the island. So, there we were, aware that we were landing on an island that was inhabited by adult men who were convicted of sex offences but not sentenced as yet. They were in charge of the long boats and we had to entrust our lives and wellbeing to them, even though we knew they might well resent our presence and, with good reason, might loathe our roles. After all, we were there to protect the children on the island and to monitor the men's activity in the hopes of protecting the children and vulnerable adults, as well as being a source of support to the now convicted, in denial and unrepentant sex offenders.

They did their job and got us onto the island safely, but they did not relish or celebrate our arrival. They felt intruded upon as if their space was invaded, which indeed it was. We were uninvited guests, there to protect children at the command of the British government which had dominion over the island that had become the safe haven for the mutiny on the Bounty survivors.

Pitcairn Islands is a very unusual and beautiful place. The fruits are larger than life and ever so colourful and pretty, and it is my view they even tasted nicer than the same fruits that I have eaten on other islands and in other countries. The sea surrounding the island roared like a million lions in severe pain all the time. The sound was strong and enduring to a degree of absolutely overpowering all other sounds. It took me weeks to get used to the sound of the sea bashing against itself to and fro, time and time again. I never thought it would ever become just background noise, but it did, and on leaving the island I was surprised that I had grown so used to the sound of the sea that it became a comforting deep soothing echo that reminded me that we were a part of the much greater experience, dwelling like tiny little atoms in a vast number of molecules. It took me weeks to adjust to *not* hearing the sound of the sea. I felt an emptiness, as though a good and talkative friend had left me in a room with silent observers.

The most amazing thing about staying on Pitcairn Islands for three months with a population of forty-seven people and a handful of professionals is that it allowed me an opportunity to be with myself, in the open air, through the forest and bushes of the islands and on rare occasions at the top of rocks looking down at the roaring sea. Although the people on the island were up early and often at the door by seven in the morning, they were also in their homes by half past seven most evenings. This left me with a great deal of time to exercise, relax, meditate and contemplate the purpose of life and just who I was and who I was becoming. Other social workers who had spent three months on the islands had reported that they became very bored and frustrated, due to the lack of television, radio and socialising outlets, not to mention *not* hearing from friends and family on a regular basis. For me, this was a nice neat slice of heaven. All that space to be close to my creator in a land that was always hot and beautiful to look at, with people who held a unique window into my history of slavery. The history of the Pitcairn Islands is that Captain Bligh was on a journey to gather breadfruit in order to feed the slaves in the West Indies. During that journey, Captain Bligh experienced assault by his own men, many of whom were not willing participants on the journey because in times long ago sailors were often petty or serious criminals, those who could not feed themselves or those that had to hide from the authorities, hence many were disgruntled before even starting the journey and several would die before their return.

Some of the reluctant sailors on the ship known as the Bounty decided to take control of the ship and they overpowered the loyal cabin crew and took over the ship. In their wisdom, or lack of it, however, they decided not to kill Captain Bligh but placed him in a small boat and left him to the fate of the sea. Captain Bligh was indeed an exceptional sailor and somehow managed to survive and find his way home to England from the depths of the South Pacific Ocean, and on his safe arrival back in England, he reported the fact that he had been overthrown and his ship stolen. The mutineers decided to take no chances on the ship ever being found, so once they came across the small island now known as Pitcairn, they ceremonially burned the Bounty, so that it would never be found and their hideaway on the new-found island would always be safe from any who might search for them. To this day, there is a ceremony of burning a makeshift Bounty to mark the experience of the creation of their new home on Pitcairn Island.

So, you see, in the same way that being press ganged was a life-changing event for those criminals whose ancestors were now sailors and exiles, my stay on Pitcairn was life-changing for me by giving me the chance to think about just who I was and where I belonged in the universe. I became aware of the fact that I was truly not alone. I had an opportunity to get closer to this inner source that was greater than I and that which kept me company through daily thoughts, contemplation and meditation. I had space to be just who I am without judgement from the outer world, yet I felt a connection to times long past and in particular those who suffered and died in slavery, those whose names we will never know. It felt like poetic justice that here I was, on this island where sailors had been on a voyage to gather breadfruit seeds so that the slave masters in the Caribbean would have a cheap source of food to nourish their slaves; a black woman in a very powerful position, a social worker here to keep children safe and work alongside the authorities. I felt my purpose on Pitcairn island was to bring about a balance within history and to evidence that those that died in the middle passage, did not die in vain. I would walk through the bushes all alone and the older women would comment: 'How come you feel so brave to walk alone in the bushes, when the outer world perceives our men as so dangerous?'. I would respond 'I am never alone, there is a greater force that is always with me.' Indeed, I felt the energy of my African ancestors with me and the power of the Most High, which filled me with such confidence and bravery. I have often been described as courageous, but the courage is not mine, I have merely borrowed it from a greater source. The experience of Pitcairn Islands taught me that you never know where life is going to take you and sometimes opportunities open doors that allow you to develop aspects of yourself, but to do this one has to take chances and plan to make the most of them. My only expectation was that I would grow and hopefully come away from the experience knowing things I had not previously known. The surprising fact for me was that so many things were familiar yet different. The fruits were the same as in Jamaica. On seeing the fruits, I felt like I had been transported to the land of the giants. The coconuts, papayas, and many of the other fruits were so much bigger but tasted the same; and some were sweeter. The biggest surprise was the language of the natives who were said to be of Tahitian and English descent, yet they spoke a Jamaican dialect that I could understand and converse in to some degree. There was I, far from home, in a strange land and yet I felt more connected to those people than I do to the English people I was born and raised with. I felt like I had found a piece of my history and that I belonged. It is an amazing thing to be so far away from home and still to feel so culturally connected to a place and people one has never visited before. I was reminded of what I had previously read about soul journeys and the idea that maybe when we die, our bodies stop existing, but our souls live on and the energy of our spirit can still be experienced by people, places and things. I was sure that I was feeling the spiritual energy of those I had previously been connected to who had also passed this way or that maybe my soul had passed this way in another life and I was here to regather the pieces in order to help me with my universal journey.

I left Pitcairn Islands as a much fitter and healthier person, having enjoyed all that fresh fish, fruit and food and also the sunshine. As there were so many empty hours I also exercised along with others and alone. The experience on Pitcairn taught me that although I had routine, I never really knew what the next day would bring and therefore I had to be ready to adjust and manage new experiences. I learnt to embrace flexibility. The three months on this tropical island taught me that it is so very important to accept change and to finds ways to make that change work to your advantage, for without that ability one is at risk of never achieving one's potential or really expressing one's true self.

# Chapter 3

## The Power of Being in Grace

The power of being in grace refers to a state of constant awareness of the presence of the Most High—yet no, it does not simply mean that, it means something far more profound than that.

On researching different philosophies on the explanation of God, from Yoruba original African beliefs, Islamic practice to Christianity there is a big struggle to elaborate on the being or the essence of the Most High. Some original Egyptian writings don't even bother with the struggle to explain the unexplainable but are content to perceive this infinite unbounded source as unnameable, but not intangible.

I see this wonderful source, or force, as I see the connections between my fingernails and my stomach, or any other part of the body. My fingernails and my stomach are, in a way, separate, yet they are the same, a part of the same body, made up of the same stuff, born of the same beginnings.

In the same way as all the body parts are one, I perceive that God and man are one. We are the very same particles in a different form. It is my view that the Most High, energy, universal force, God, is indeed all that we are and has implanted in us all that the God force is.

Let me elaborate. Just as one strand of hair can hold the genetic history of the whole body and can be a source of identification if need be, we, all living and unliving things (as everything extends from something once living, to take shape and change form at some stage, it must have been live

Molecules and particles, not necessarily organic) are like the single strands of hair or particles of the Most High.

To me, the higher force is very much like the pure water that is easily diluted. Take a drink of white rum, if water is added to this, it becomes easier to swallow, yet it is the rum that intoxicates you not the water. God is similar. We are all made up of the pure water but throughout life we contaminate it with negative energy.

Let's be a little more specific and imagine that thoughts are the pure waters that run through our minds. Each thought can be impregnated with a positive energy or a negative energy; remember, if water is thought then thought is pure until we add another ingredient to it, such as an emotional charge, or an intention or a strong feeling. Thoughts are as powerful as the energy you give them, as they are able to hold the substance of God that we have likened to water, for the want of a better illustration. Like water the force of God is fluid and can also be still, with strong waves and low soft gentle waves. Under certain circumstances water can overwhelm you, hit you with such force or soothe the deepest pain. The energy of the Most High can achieve this and so much more, because unlike water, the Most High has no boundary or beginning or end. There is no substance or situation that the Most High cannot penetrate.

So, if I am the Most High and you are the Most High and so are the flowers, trees, and all that is, why are we not aware of this and why are we unable to make things manifest the way the Lord made the earth and the heavens manifest? The answer is simple yet extremely complex. Here is the simple version. The Lord is not the Most High. Remember everything is ultimately the Most High, yet the Lord is of the Most High in manifestation. In other words, the Most High is the pure water and the Lord is the other substance mixed with it. Still not clear? Here is the definition in layman's terms. The word Lord can be read as the word law or universal patterns of enfoldment, so if the universe is perceived as the Most High, then the law or patterns of enfoldment must be something created by the Most High. Hence, the law or Lord is of the Most High but is not all that the Most High is. Like the fingernail and the stomach, they are one and the same but with different functions, from the same source.

You and I have the same ability to create aspects of our body—for example, depending on how much we eat we can in some cases define our shape. We can develop patterns of reactions to certain things depending on how we consciously or unconsciously programme our minds to respond. In other words, last year I drank some certain brand of fizzy white wine which made me sick. Every time I consider drinking it, I feel as though I will be sick. What has this got to do with the Lord creating the universe? Well, as you wish it, so shall it be. The Most High desired the universe to be created and the aspect of the Most High, known as the Lord, created it. In the same way, my mind decided that the wine makes me sick, so the stomach reacts accordingly each time I think of it.

So how does this comparison relate to the idea that we are God and God is we? I like to see God as an energy, a force, a being that has recreated itself in many different forms with all of its qualities intact. However, like the rum that has been watered down, we do not have the intense force of the original source, unless we become conscious of it. Why? Because the Most High said, "I have made man in my own image and given free will to all." We have talked of the infinite connection between man and the force of the Most High. Now what of free will?

It is my opinion that the understanding and acceptance of free will tips the balance between the pure and impure water of the Most High within our very being. Earlier we spoke of positive and negative thoughts. If we were to take the quote of the Most High, we could say it another way: "I have given existence to all and they have the choice to know that they are I and I am them. If they choose not to identify themselves as a part of this body, then they may dwell in isolation from all that the source has to offer. If, on the other hand, they become aware that we are one and the same, then they will know their power and utilise it for their greater good, backed and supported by the main source."

Let me give you an analogy. If your brain failed to recognise that you had legs which could take your body about the place quite easily, then your body would have a struggle getting about and indeed would have to drag the legs along, whether it was conscious of them or not. Another example, Doctors will often enquire on the health status of your parents, not because you are doomed to the same illnesses, but since you are of the same make-up your bodies might react in the same way, given a certain set of circumstances. If you became conscious that your father was skilled at, say, playing an instrument, it would not be too far-fetched to believe that you could train yourself to play also, even though you might never be as good as him. That is not a very good example because I believe God has given us all the capacity within our individual imaginations to achieve and create any and everything we can. However, we need to know deep within us that we are the source of this creation because, ultimately, we are no different from the Most High, just limited in our ability like a toddler whose legs are too short for them to keep up with an adult. It is not that they do not have the speed or the ability but the equipment that they have access to is not as vast as the adult's.

Knowing that we are one with the Most High allows us to connect with a power that is not diluted but pure and capable of creating any and everything we can allow ourselves to imagine, by accessing the will of God. Free will means we have been given the grace to believe anything we want to, but to believe something that is not of the Highest will not afford us the power to manifest as the Most High does. If we only believe in our connection, just a little bit, it will work for us, but only a little bit. You see, you are in charge of the fluidity of this power and a little belief allows for a little flow and small manifestations. To know that you are a pro-creator with the Most High allows you to expand your desire, just as my fingernails will grow without waiting for my mind to consciously give the order. If we are aware of our God force and abide by the law/Lord, we will manifest all manner of things easily and effortlessly. But wait—what is this about the law/ Lord. Why is it not enough to know that I am one with the creator? The truthful answer is *because you have been given free will*; the law is a way of knowing what choice you have truly made and what source you wish to be aligned with. This is to do with our thoughts and our constant awareness of being able to choose to be in a state of grace. And it also has to do with the idea of unconscious and negative attraction.

What we spend our time and energy thinking about will manifest in our lives, the thoughts are the creators of our next experiences, sometimes the thoughts will bring things about very quickly and at other times it could take years or months. the timing of when our thoughts will become reality depends on a lot of things, such as how much power, time and energy we gave those thoughts or if the mind is already in the process of bringing a certain thing in your life that would clash with the manifestation of the current thought. As you think or imagine situations in your head, they leave a mould of what needs to become the outer picture in your life, and then the ink starts to fill the mould, by bringing the imagined situation into your life. remember you always have control because you have free will and you can create a different mould and fill it with fluorescent ink and then watch bright and wonderful things manifest in your life. the mould is the thoughts in your mind the ink is the elaboration on these thoughts or the finer details which is created by using your imagination.

Most of the time, our thoughts pass through our minds without us being aware of them or they are a response to a feeling, fantasy or fear and we often forget that even those thoughts are creating our future experiences and will manifest in our life's. this could be described as unconscious thoughts and the fact that such thoughts are left, undisturbed they have the power to build big moulds and to grow enormously, without interruption, that's why it is very important that we make efforts to become aware of those hidden or silent thoughts that we may be harbouring and at least hold enough conscious thoughts to weaken and counteract any negative or unconscious thoughts.

# Chapter 4.

## Unconscious and Negative Attraction.

Over the past few years I have noticed that the type of men I have been meeting have all been very nice and warm and friendly, when I was in their presence. However, as soon as I was out of sight it was as though I was also out of mind. I told myself that this was because they were mainly two-timing, good for the nothing users, who were not interested in meaningful relationships. That was, of course, after I got over the self-defeating fantasies and ideas that something must be wrong with *me.* Then I reflected on the matter spiritually and asked myself just what these relationships were trying to tell me and where in my life had I failed to give attention to something that was out of mind as soon as it was out of sight. I considered why I had been attracting this type of man into my life and what was being mirrored back to me through meeting and relating to these men. I thought of family members and asked myself, had I neglected them, or was there someone I should be paying more attention to? After hours of painful soul-searching I could not come up with anything. As I was ready to retire and go to bed for the night, with no solutions, the usual thought of 'oh I have not added any more information to the book tonight, so I'll do it tomorrow', crossed my mind—and there it was. It was not a person or a relative that I was neglecting to relate to. I was failing to fulfil my commitment to writing this book. I had neglected to relate to my literal spiritual task, and life was reflecting this back to me perfectly. Writing a book, especially on this subject is a very intimate task and indeed

I do have a relationship with this creation, which I had been neglecting. Hence, it has taken over five years to complete.

The law of ATTRACTION was ensuring that this was manifesting in my life, whether I was conscious of it or not. Hence, the lesson was learnt—attend to the relationship with my book, and the man in my life would attend to me. I then remembered the number of times, I had heard guys say, "I was going to ring you, but then I noticed the time and it was too late." I would respond by saying it's never too late to ring me, but my thoughts were, well that's a feeble excuse. Yet there I was relating to my book, or rather not relating, in the very same way. That night I took up my work diary and wrote on the next three weeks of dates that I would write something of the book each night, until it became a habit or was completed.

Having grown tired of potential partners who would ultimately fail to meet my needs, I decided to change my mind set in the hope of attracting a more genuine and permanent partner. Just by thinking differently and ultimately valuing myself a little bit more, I have been able to attract men with different and more long-lasting desires towards me. This switch in my mindset opened me up to meeting guys who were different from the previous ones, and so I enjoyed different subject matters and events that have left me feeling more fulfilled and satisfied in my later relationships. And all because I decided to take responsibility for what I had previously been experiencing.

Thoughts are powerful things whether you are conscious of them or not and the law of attraction will ensure that what we are putting out there, be it in thought, action or deed, will manifest in our lives and come right back at us. The difficulty is that if we are unconscious of what we are subliminally creating, then we have less, or no, opportunity to be aware of why these things are manifesting in our lives and we miss the chance to actively reverse the reaction and address the issue.

When I notice a pattern of things happening in my life and I cannot put it down to other people's behaviour, then I get to thinking it must be something I am creating. I do not spend too much time worrying about why I am creating it—that would involve getting into self-blame or feelings of guilt and that is a waste of my time and ability. I prefer to try and discover what is being revealed to me and then I remain open to the answer, even if it is difficult to accept. Sometimes I cannot work it out, but I trust that once I am willing, spirit will help me, by showing me a sign or allowing the answer to pop into my head, as it did with the book. The rest is up to me to take action to reverse the negative thoughts and messages that I have been consciously or unconsciously creating.

It is amazing what happens when we actively change our thoughts or strive to create a new positive habit that leads to conscious thoughts about what we want. What might happen next is very scary and very exciting. The man that I am really interested in may well become more attentive and that would be great, or he may disappear out of my life as it may not be his role to be attentive to me. This is where I will need to be brave and strong as I do not wish to lose him, but as I change he may not be able to stay. People come into your life to fulfil certain purposes and his may have been to give me an experience of being ignored in order for me to have the revelation that I should be attending to and focusing on the book. He may have a wider remit and more lessons to teach me; in which case the relationship will continue until I have learnt all the relevant spiritual and earthly lessons from him and he from me.

Of course, this is not as simple and straightforward as it sounds. After all, we are talking about the interactions of human beings, which involve motivation, habits, needs and desires. Some of us stay together out of habit and fear of change, even when it does not feel right to us. Others are motivated to succeed against all odds, because that is what they do in relationships and they are determined not to let go, maybe because it would leave them vulnerable or spoil an image, or sadly because it would cost them too much financially and emotionally. Recently my brother was talking to me about how some men think, in relation to commitments they have made in their minds or at a church altar when getting married. My brother explained that for some men it is more important for them to keep to their word once they have committed to something, not because they are honourable but more because that is what they have decided and therefore they will not change their minds, or deviate from the plan, even it is no longer works. To change their minds about something they have vowed to do may leave them feeling that they have failed at the challenge of being true to their word, which would make them feel less of a man. If they did break their vow, they might end up feeling that they could not trust themselves to commit to anything or anyone else in the future, ultimately leaving them feeling a sense of vulnerability and low self-worth. Therefore, once they have made up their mind they stick to the path because it is more comfortable and safer than being flexible in the light of new information or experiences and changing direction.

Many of us hide behind that old notion called love. We tell ourselves that although we know on some real level that the relationship is neither healthy nor good for either party, we hold on because we love. I have decided that if I am in a relationship that leaves me feeling constantly empty, wanting, and void of affection, or is causing me pain and distress along with a feeling of confusion and sadness, in fact, if I am in a relationship that does not enhance my wellbeing and allow me to feel valued, then I will decide to continue to love that person as I do, but from a distance from which they can no longer influence my life negatively. You see, you do not have to stop loving the person, but the destructive relationship has to stop in order for you to thrive, and love can exist whether you interact with the person or not. It's often better to love at a distance, for when you love at distance there is less room for anger and hate of the person who once brought you joy and happiness. It's often easier to let go of a person with an understanding that you do not have to stop loving them. Many broken-hearted people suffer because they are struggling with trying to stop loving the person. Love is not like that, you cannot turn it off or on as you desire. You did not choose it, it chose you, and once love is born it lives until it dies. Some of us have tried to murder love through arguments and deceit, but often all we end up achieving is 'distance love' tainted by negative experiences.

There is something graceful and comforting about holding the love of a person in your heart—not that that is the kindest thing you could do—rather than continue a destructive and painful relationship with them. In my view to, love at a distance despite the reason for parting is the essence of genuine unconditional love and often deep meaningful friendships are born out of this. In order to survive all the complexities of love and relationships, we need to remain flexible and skilled at finding ways to cope with our lived experiences without destroying ourselves or allowing others to destroy us in the process. None of this is easy but it's so crucial to our emotional physical and spiritual wellbeing.

In my opening paragraph I commented that over the past few years I have noticed a pattern in my relationships of non-attentiveness from partners. It really does not matter when you notice it, it is just important that you do notice it and take action to change and adjust it if necessary or desirable. The very next day after reflecting on the pattern of my relationships, two guys who could be classed as ex-partners contacted me. The first sent me a text saying 'Hi.'. I had not seen him for some two years and was tempted not to respond but curiosity got the better of me, so I rang him later that day. He was an ex-boyfriend who I just adored, but at the time he was in a meaningful relationship and had no intention of leaving her. We then met some seven years later when he was in another relationship and had more children. He was very committed to his children, but he wanted to have an affair with me. I wanted a man of my very own, so it never worked out. When he called me the next day after my reflections on the pattern of my relationships, he said that his relationship was over and that he was about to close the deal on a new property he was buying. He had left the children and the woman. I expressed sympathy in relation to his plight and wished him all the best. He promised to visit soon and I left it there. I was grateful to spirit for the message of acknowledgment that something was changing in my life. It was not an excuse, however, to rescue him from his 'aloneness'. Two hours later, I received another call from another ex-guy—Wow! The day was becoming very revealing. He just said: "Hi, how are you? I am just seeing how you are." I thanked him and had a trivial conversation about how my day was going, we said goodbye and left it at that. At no point in the day did I hear from the man that I was currently interested in, so I figured I should give thanks for the messages received and just keep writing. Who knows? Maybe this current man would just drift out of my life, or maybe more connection with my book was needed before he could respond. After all, the other guys had been around for years and this one had only been in my life for months. Gentle new plants need more time to grow before they can show their true colours, so patience is required, and maybe his path in my life is about a different message and not related to the old pattern that I have recognised.

The Biblical quote that people are in our lives for a reason and season is so true. We have a duty to ourselves to try and work out what the reason, lesson or purpose is for those in our lives so that we do not waste vital life lessons or miss warnings and opportunities that could enhance our lives. We do need to learn to think about negative and positive attraction and as we think about these things, the lessons will reveal themselves to us.

# Chapter 5

## Direct Messages from Spirit

When we hear the word spirit, we often become cautious and scared—evil things such as bad ghosts and entities taking over someone's body come to mind. That is the legacy of hype—the media telling us and selling us a load of negativity in order to make successful horror films or sell sensational stories. The truth is the Bible, the Quran and other religious text have spoken of the spirit coming to prophets and others over many thousands of years.

I believe that we are all a part of infinite spirit, so we all have the ability to connect and experience spirit on many different levels. Some call this clairvoyance, others refer to an inner knowing or a soul connection. Either way, the fact that we as humans are able to tap into something outside of ourselves that can reveal information not yet evident is a fact, and I now want to talk to you about such things.

I see myself as a well-disciplined woman who likes to keep certain aspects of my life quite separate with clear boundaries. My day job at the moment is that of Local Authority Designated Officer (LADO -dealing with allegations against Professionals) Manager where I am in charge of ensuring that children are protected from abuse at the hands of professionals. I also train professionals and community workers in child protection and safeguarding issues. I know in my mind that spirit guides me in this work, but I never reveal anything about spirit while doing my day job unless, of course, I am dealing with the subject matter as part of my work, and indeed this is sometimes the case.

Lately we have had several cases of children being deemed to be witches by rogue pastors or parents who think that evil has come into their lives due to the fact that a child in the household is possessed by an evil spirit. Some families will take grave steps to rid a child of such a possession and they truly believe that a family can be cursed in this way. To rid a child of an evil possession, the family and or rogue pastor/faith leader may resort to acts of burning, drowning, beating and even killing the child. This, in my view and the view of British law, is child abuse and is totally unacceptable under any circumstances. Children are to be protected and loved at all times. My spiritual view is that evil does exist, insomuch as it is a manifestation of the lack of love in one's life and may cause a person to feel very fearful and void of protection. The idea of evil holds no power in relation to good and the love that we receive from the Most High. Some of us would beg to differ, I am sure, and we will explore such views a little later. As a professional child protection worker, I perceive it as my duty to remain ethical and only do my job when I am at work. I do not share with my colleagues on a regular basis what I am sharing with you now. This is for a number of reasons. They may think me to be some religious fanatic or that I am depending on some other type of assessment outside of social work theory when dealing with families. The truth is, I am conscious that I am never separate from my spirit, so I work within the parameters of the status quo knowing that I am guided by spirit always. It's a bit like believing in the healing powers of prayer, yet it is important to continue taking conventional medicines. Spirit is wise enough to make best use of all aspects of healing.

I have spoken of my connection to spirit and the messages that I have received. Even though spirit has made every effort to connect with me from childhood, I am still amazed at what is revealed about people's lives through me as a channel of spirit. I want to tell you something of that in order to evidence the power of spirit and the way thoughts work with us and through us. I must confess I do not fully understand how it works, but experience has forced me to accept that there is more to our capabilities and our world. We may learn more about in time or we may remain ignorant as to how spirit is able to be so creative and innovative, so that experiences in our lives are woven together like a complex tapestry, according to our needs and creative thoughts.

Over the past eighteen months, I have been working as a social worker in a very leafy and pretty part of England. I have been fortunate to work with a skilled group of lovely people who have somewhat of an appreciation for spirituality, and during some evenings out at the local pub, some members of the team asked me to give them a spiritual reading. As usual, I made no promises and said I would only give them what I received from spirit. While sipping brandy, team members would give me their hand, I would ask them to relax and then I would connect to spirit by asking Jesus to be with me and I would also relax. I would get pictures or words that would just pop into my head, as well as an energy or feeling from the image of the person who had popped into my head. Sometimes the words and feelings made very little sense to me, but I would share them with the person before me and often it would make perfect sense to them. When giving a reading, I like to hold the person's hands, even though I can get messages without holding their hands. I just find that if I hold their hands, they remain focused on the reading and they feel safe and comforted.

One woman was feeling particularly distressed and asked if she could come around to my home for a reading. We met up, I explained the process and I held her hand, I told her that she would have a pregnancy in 18 months and that she would have a baby girl. She informed me that she had two boys and could not afford another child and that this was not in her and her husband's plan. They wanted to move, and he was seeking more lucrative work. However, I insisted that this was what spirit was telling me. I have learnt to ignore the earthly, logical or practical things that people tell me when I am giving them readings and simply stick to the messages I am receiving, as I am aware of just how amazing, innovative and creative spirit can be, so in spite of worldly restrictions and practical issues, spirit has a way of making things happen and work out for individuals that would be way beyond anything they could imagine for themselves. Hence, I offer the message and invite the receiver of the reading to accept it if they choose or reject the idea if it seems too far-fetched. However, I remind them that the mind is creative and powerful and if we open up to the power of spirit, great things can happen once the spiritual energy unites with our earthly energy through the power of thought, firm belief and appropriate action.

Some nine months later this lady, who had now left the workplace, contacted me and said that she was pregnant and was told she was having a girl. She explained that by the time the child was born it would be 18 months since I gave her the reading. I was amazed, as I always am when spirit evidences that it can foresee what will unfold into the future. In spite of the accuracy of the reading, I always tell people that they are in charge of their own future and have the power to change anything they have heard, as they have free will. I sincerely believe this.

Another woman was given a reading in a pub and I informed her that her husband would get a new job far away and would have to commute, amongst other things she was told. That night she went home all excited, wanting to tell her husband of the prediction about his career. He was also keen to share some exciting news, so they enthusiastically spent time saying let me go first, no let me. Then he went first and announced that he had been told that he had a job just outside London and would have to commute for some two hours from the leafy quiet part of England to get there on a daily basis. She said, "I know! This clairvoyant told me about it this evening." On hearing this news, I felt so humbled and honoured to be blessed with the reality that spirit had chosen me as a channel of these messages that touch and impact so positively in people's lives and give them hope that they are not alone or without support. I simply say, 'Thank you Lord for the blessing.' and I strive to fulfil my purpose in life, by asking for guidance as to what I should be doing to help myself, my family and my fellow man, woman and child, while I can.

I share this with you in order to help you to appreciate that spirit is alive and active, and I believe this is the case in all our lives. Some of us are just more tuned into it than others and all of us can have a wonderful connection with spirit if we choose to and we are able to discard the negative emotions, thoughts and unconscious limitations that often get in our way from time to time.

Now the act of spirit communicating with me has always been fascinating and surprising. As a child, I was conscious of the ability to know what would unfold in some situations and grew used to receiving clues about imminent events such as the time when my friend and I took the textbooks out of the cupboard when the teacher was reading a story to the class, at the age of six or seven. We were caught in the act, a silly act really, as the teacher could see us crawling around on the floor and going behind her to the cupboard. The class teacher, a small Scottish woman with dark hair, a round face and plump cheeks, Mrs Owen, promptly sent us to the headmaster's office to receive a severe telling off and time to feel appropriately embarrassed. My friend was really worried and very tearful. I was very cool and calm, as deep within I knew the headmaster would not be there. I told my friend this and she said: "Yes he is. Look his red car is outside." So, we went to the office, the secretary told us to sit outside the office and wait. I must confess at that point I became worried. Then the secretary appeared and announced: "You are very lucky—the headmaster had to leave early, so go back to class and don't do it again."

My friend looked out of the window again as we returned to our class and this time the little red car was not there. She asked me how I knew and I just smiled and said I told you. We never attempted to steal books again though, as the trip to the headmaster's office was scary for us as little children.

So even though at a young age I had some understanding of spirit working in my life and I was aware that I could see into people's lives on occasion, I never thought that the power was mine, because I could not control it or decide when I would get an insight, and to this day I still do not believe the power is mine.

As I became older and started to give readings, spirit worked with me in different ways. As a child, I was just conscious of knowing stuff with no idea of how I knew these things. It was like knowledge popping into my head without warning or any other identifiable thing. However, as I became older and started to deliberately try to give readings, I became aware of pictures in my thoughts, almost like live films playing out. I could see people in their childhood, in past situations, accompanied by emotions of that person at that time, and I could see the surrounding people with them. As I described what I could see, people would tell me that they were able to recall that incident. Sometimes I am able to describe people's homes or workplaces in great detail, to my utter surprise. What became apparent to me was that by understanding situations and incidents of people's past experiences, I was able to help them gain insight into how those situations had shaped their lives, habits, emotions and beliefs about themselves now, for better or worse. I was able to understand the dynamics of their emotional journey through insight into their actual past experiences, or that of others around them. Sometimes I would see people's current experience and how they were coping with it.

If I were to name this phenomenon, I would call it clairvoyant psychotherapy, as it takes an individual's past experiences and relates them to the current emotional charge or behaviour that they are exhibiting today. Rather than taking years to uncover the real significant stuff in a person's life, the spiritual path just brings up the salient stories or episodes and relates them to the impact on the individual today.

Spirit is good, and I think it only reveals to people what they need to know and what they can handle. I have had people beg me to tell them what will happen in their relationships and if it is good for them, but I can only give them what spirit gives me. As I have grown up with spirit and I have learnt to value it, I never have the desire to tell them what they want to hear or to deceive them. I take my partnership with spirit very seriously, to such a degree that if for any reason I do not feel like giving someone a reading, then I won't, and I don't even feel the need to justify that. When people come to me for readings and I charge a fee, I make it clear that they are in fact paying for my time and energy, and not for the spiritual experience, because I could not begin to put a price on what happens in those moments and no one would be able to afford it, as it is, in fact, priceless.

Most of the readings I do are done for fun, or for a drink if I am in a pub with friends, and all of the time I enjoy the experience and feel energised afterwards. Of late, I am discovering that I am doing more and more predictive readings, which I do not feel too comfortable with, as I strongly believe that we make our own path in life and our futures are not predestined. I think we have the capacity to *shape* our futures according to the power of our thoughts and our commitment to work in line with the universal laws. However, lately, the readings have been able to reveal what will unfold in people's lives in months or years to come. I guess some people require support in helping them to work towards their goals by having spirit back them up with their desires and this is what I am revealing. In other words, maybe people are creating their own futures but not believing in them strongly enough until someone like me comes along and says I can see that in their future. This I am not sure about, as I have examples of people being in total distress and I have told them things they did not wish to hear at that time and these things have come to pass.

I recall a situation many years ago when a woman came to me having just lost a child and broken up with the would-be father. She was totally distressed and angry with me. All she wanted to know was if she would survive the tremendous pain she was feeling right now and have a happier future, with or without a partner. I informed her that she would be happy and would marry in the space of a few short months and that he would be of a particular racial type that was different from hers. Well this did not fit with who she perceived herself to be. She found it quite funny to hear this and thanked me for bringing a smile to her face, but she laughed it off. This woman was married within the short timescale that I mentioned to a man of an ethnic type she had never dated before, and she was very happy. Sometimes when we are feeling totally forlorn and bereft of any hope, we just need someone to hope for us. I think spirit knows this and helps individuals to create thoughts and possibilities in their minds that become positive thoughts, whether they are alert to them or not, on a daily basis. This brings about a different and more fulfilling experience in their lives. I call these those times when spirit holds us by the hand and leads us to constructive and creative thoughts that impact on our lives positively. Others might describe it as the 'walking in the sand' poem, when Jesus is said to carry us at our weakest moments. My mother might have said, "The mind and body may be weak, but the spirit is willing", this is a quote from the bible that she often made reference to. I think the spirit wills good things for us in every sense of the word and is willing to give us direct messages if we are willing to hear.

My mother and father's Silver Jubilee Wedding (25 years) anniversary party, with me and all my parents children, in the 70s.

# Chapter 6

## When the Blessings Start to Pour

Many of these 'how to embrace spirituality' books will tell you a great deal about how to bring yourself into the realm of prosperity and peace, but few offer guidance on what to do once you begin to receive it. It is crucially important that you know how to handle your blessings, as this will set the course for the rest of your manifestations.

As psychologists and philosophers will tell you, it is very important to understand our history in order to be able to move beyond our past. This is also true of our personal history, and our mind and soul know this. Many of us will be able to identify with the experience of repeating past situations over and over again. This is echoed in sayings like 'why do I always meet idlers or partners who hurt me?'; others will know that if ever they have a sum of useful money they somehow manage to squander it and end up struggling financially as usual. Repeating negative life experiences may be about a number of factors, such as self-worth or the lack of self-worth, or maybe fear of succeeding when others around us do not seem to have the same level of opportunities. We may fear that if we excel too much then we will become too different to fit in with those we see as peers and loved ones, and most common of the hindrances is the idea that achievements and positive change are not for us but for another set of people.

I think the most devastating reason and cause of not progressing beyond our past experiences is due to the inner force that wants to understand what happened to us in the past and how and why we went through such pain as children and younger people. We try to achieve this by recreating the painful situation or relationship in order to make sense of it from the stage of life we are now in. For example, if we were raised by a mother who never prioritised our needs or a father that belittled our achievements, we may well find a partner, boss or flatmate who treats us in a similar fashion, and again we go through a situation that entails us experiencing emotional rejection and/or a belittling situation. While we experience this, we are hoping that somehow, we will be able to grasp an insight into why or how someone could treat us like that, and maybe we even hope to respond to the negative treatment in a manner that protects us from the past pain and present distress that we are going through.

This re-experiencing of previous negative situations is often done on an unconscious level as a coping strategy for unresolved past inner conflicts. There comes a stage in our lives when we recognise that we have been through a similar situation before, but somehow we cannot stop ourselves, so now we are conscious of our recreation of the negative experience, but we still allow ourselves to go through it with the same motivations of making it right this time, or learning to understand how or why others would hurt us in this way—hence the question 'why do I always find myself in this situation?'.

My answer to that question is that what we are actually doing is something I would call *emotional self-harm*. Self-harm usually involves a self-inflicted injury to the physical body such as cutting or taking drugs. Emotional self-harm causes scars on our inner feelings and ultimately makes it more difficult to heal in the long run as we keep re-opening the same old wounds. My motto is, leave the fixing of cars to car mechanics and if it is not working, find yourself a good mechanic or get a new car. In the meantime, use some other mode of transport. In human terms, this means when our internal historical emotional system requires repair, then we should seek appropriate assistance via coaching, therapy, self-help books and techniques, or prayer, depending on what works for you. What we should *not* do is to keep driving the broken car until it drops. Or, in other words, we only damage ourselves further by repeating past hurts over and over again. When we see that we are in a recurring cycle, then we should park it up for a while and make a decision as to what we will do about it.

My words of guidance are, once you become aware of a repeating pattern, then stop it—either leave the relationship, move out of the shared

Apartment with the abusive flatmates, or find a new position away from the exploiting boss, or simply let go of the personal battle of trying to understand it or fix it. Whatever you do, find a way of letting go of the situation that reintroduces the past pains and emotional upsets. By doing this, you will be freed up to embrace your future and start to begin to really hold on to your new achievements. Of course, it is never this simple, as the people we are relating to are often also trying to relive a past experience on some level and require us to play a certain role. The important thing to remember is that we do not have the capacity to change others and can only change ourselves. The amazing thing about taking time out to work on yourself is that is ultimately impacts on others. In particular, making a personal shift in your emotional attachments to past experiences will cause others to have to relate to you differently, which in effect means they will also have to make a shift in *their* personal emotional attachments. If the person you are interacting with is unable to make such a shift, they will leave your life, and this will be their way of letting go of the situation this time. Such people will often find someone else to help them re-enact the previous emotional pain that they unconsciously wish to struggle with.

Previous struggles are often a blessing and have the power to equip us with the inner strength to deal with new struggles if we are wise enough to appreciate that we survived the past and can do so again, even if we don't understand quite how we did this.

So for those of us who are able to accept that there are many things we will never really work out or understand, in terms of why and how harsh things or negative experiences could have happened to us, but are prepared to move forward knowing that we are now in control of our futures, doors will open and great things can be achieved. The task will always be to remain in the positive can-do mode and not to slip back into old patterns that tell us that we *still are* that hurt and distressed child or younger person who can never have the good things.

What you think and believe about your blessings and new-found abundance will influence how future events will become apparent in your life, through your power of thought. When good things happen to us, many of us have a habit of saying things like it is too good to be true or I can't believe it. Remember your thoughts are powerful and creative. So be careful about how you receive your goods and always remember to

Say thank you to the Most High or the higher part of you, in a genuine manner. You only need to say this to yourself.

As important as it is to remain humble so that you are always aligned with grace, it is also important to know that you deserve all the good you get as you are a God-like creator and allowed to benefit from all you create. Look at the positive manifestations in your live as things you have made and are pleased with. This can be done gracefully as long as you refrain from comparing yourself to others or presuming that your creations or prosperity make you better than others. This may sound simple but, in this very competitive world that we live in, it is not easy, as success is often measured by the failure of others. The only thing you are in competition with is yourself, so your successes and failures are all your own. Be gentle with yourself when you have not achieved your goals and kind to yourself when you do. By doing this, you develop a mind-set of humbleness and enjoying your triumphs without creating a lot of unnecessary negative thoughts that will manifest in your future life.

The other thing that some of us tend to do once we are on a good stretch in life is to look back at our past and say, "Look at me now—when no one thought I would make anything of my life, look what I have achieved." The only thing to remember now is that you were one of the main people who went around thinking that you would not make anything of your life, so, rather than gloating, you might want to reflect on your distrust of yourself and again be gentle and kind and maybe thank your previous past and experience for equipping you to appreciate the blessings now, for without the hard times, how would we possibly know how great the goods time are?

Also, never forget the strengths you created to deal with those hard times, which will assist you in managing the good times, if you allow yourself to be a whole person and do not forget the previous crucial lessons in the unsure and scary process of survival, often against all the odds. How good are you? Just as good as you allow yourself to be, nothing less, nothing more. Again, I warn you about sharing your blessings with others as in a blink of an eye someone who does not feel too great about themselves can say something or even say nothing that leaves you feeling less than when you first started talking to them about your blessings. Then you start to think that maybe it's not so great, or who cares what you think, I am better than you, or maybe you think they are just jealous and undeserving of sharing in your joy. Either way, if you harbour such thoughts, you plant negative seeds that will ultimately impact on your life not theirs, so afford yourself some protection by only sharing your blessing with those who wish you well. The rest will see you and know that something is different and positive about you, but they will not be armed with the information or permission from you to deconstruct the wonderful creation that you have built and is currently benefiting your life. Trust that spirit will guide you in all that you do.

# Chapter 7

## Giving and Receiving

Duality and trilogy are the key to the spiritual law of giving and receiving. The Spiritual Law states, whatever you give out comes back to you like a boomerang, but sometimes not so obviously. You see as you give it out it travels and collects momentum. It may even change form, energy and strength on its journey so that, by the time it gets back to you, it may appear to be different but in essence it is just the same. You have heard the old saying about what goes around comes around. Some say that what you give out you get back tenfold. That's because it has gone out into the energetic force of the universe and developed into more of itself before it returns. What has this got to do with duality and trilogy, you may well ask? Well, let's go back a step to the possible beginning.

It is said that the Egyptians believed that in the beginning there was one, one energy, one force, one power, and that this power was all knowing and being. Absolutely nothing existed outside of itself. This force was and is intelligent and conscious of itself and all that it was—which was everything and nothing, all at the same time. The story goes that this wonderful and powerful being desired a reflection of itself and in order to create such a reflection it needed to divide itself into two, rather than one. And so, it was done. However, the side that became the reflection was not as conscious as the side that desired the reflection, yet it had every element in it to be as conscious if it so chose. In creating duality, the other half of this force had all the powers, creativity and decision-making capacities as the original half, but to be truly separate it also needed the ability to have free will. And the rest of the story, you already know. It is told in every religion, and spiritual belief. We are forever searching and trying to reconnect with that original source.

Giving and receiving is about creating. One gives, another receives, and a new situation is created. Just like birth, out of the exchange of two, the male and female, a third is developed. This is true of all situations, not just material exchange. For example, if I offer someone a gift and they accept it, a new experience is created out of that exchange, a new set of beliefs about each other comes into play and something that did not exist before now exists. Just like colours, if you mix two together, you get a third, different colour. Another way to look at it is like you and the information explored on these pages—if you feel connected to it, something new will be born and you will receive a different experience, hence the duality creates the trilogy that impacts on our lives.

On a deeper level, we also give and receive in terms of our intentions and thoughts of each other. If I give out loving caring thoughts to another, they become aware of this by my attitude towards them and they receive this vibe from me, whether they desire it or not and will most likely react accordingly. This brings us to the power of thought, which we will discuss in more depth in future chapters.

The universal law says, you cannot give more than you think you have and you cannot have more than you think you can receive. You may say, well I cannot give to another what I do not possess. However, the second part you might think is a little tricky. You may say, once someone presents me with an offer, then I will be in a position to accept it, whether I knew about it earlier or not. The truth is, all is in your possession to give and all is already yours to receive. Your response to this may be 'Yeah, right, so how come I don't have that Seven Series BMW I have always wanted, or that three-bedroom apartment near Buckingham Palace? Or how come I can't find my soul mate or have the baby I so desire etc?' Well, this is all connected to the power of thought and the universal law of attraction, including the ability to give and receive

As my mother lay on that hospital bed on a rainy Wednesday evening, I received a phone call while at work telling me she was dying and that I should get there as soon as I could. Dear Lord, I prayed, get me there in time, as I took buses and tubes to Hammersmith Hospital in London.

I arrived to find the nurses busying themselves around her. Mum had secondary cancer of the throat and now could hardly speak. On a previous visit, we spoke of death. Mum said, "I know my God will receive me, but it is what happens in the meantime that I am worried about." She went on to say that she could not stand the thought of worms eating her body. Mum knew she was dying she had worked in a hospital for some twenty years on that very type of ward with cancer patients, and indeed she had prepared for her death in line with the custom of older Caribbean people. In order to comfort and support her, I said, "You know what I believe about death, don't you? I think when you die you go into a perfect dream state and the next thing you know, you wake up as a tiny little baby, cradled in somebody's arms who will be really pleased to see you and so glad that you are healthy and well." She smiled, and in spite of her Church of England beliefs said, "That would be nice." But on that rainy Wednesday evening, mother wasn't saying much, yet she still smiled.

She had another visitor that day, a plump, mature, light-skinned black woman who worked with her at Central Middlesex hospital in Park Royal—together they fed and cared for the patients. The woman sat there, with a blue and green floral nylon headscarf folded like a triangle around her head, crying uncontrollably. I asked my mother if she would like the woman to leave. She said, "No. Let her be."

That was just like my mum. She would always allow people to do just what made them feel good or OK, as long as this was not hurting others. I was relieved when the woman left, as my coping strategy was to try and appear happy and as relaxed as possible under the circumstances. Within half an hour my mother became weaker. The nurses did all they could to make her comfortable. Mum had agreed to take part in some sort of cancer research, so they kept pricking her fingers to take blood samples as she was slipping away. She was still lucid and could answer my questions by nodding her head and saying a few words.

I noticed Mum was looking up into the corner of the ceiling; her eyes followed something from side to side. I enquired of her, "What are you looking at, Mum?" At first, she did not answer but just kept looking. Now her eyes were moving in different directions as if she was looking at a wider area of movement. I looked up too, in order to try and see what she saw, but I could see nothing but old stained, beige-painted pipes going up the wall and an empty white ceiling. I asked again, "What is it? Please tell me. I know you can see something." "Don't worry," was the response she gave me. This went on for approximately seven minutes and every now and then something would catch her eye and she would look up again.

Soon after, Mum asked me to call one of the nurses, which I did. She wanted to use the bedpan. In jest, full fun, I said to her, "I know you like your privacy, so I'll leave you to it and come back in a few minutes." She smiled and chuckled a little. On my return, five minutes later, a nurse stopped me as I was about to enter the curtain enclosure around my mother's bed. The nurse then said, "Your mother slipped away peacefully."

Well, I thought I was ready, and in that moment, I discovered I was not. Every part of my body went numb and I don't know what kept me standing, as I could not feel my legs. The woman who had taught me so much about life had gone—her body was still there, but she was not. I looked at her long and hard, and indeed she looked peaceful, as though she was sleeping. I watched her chest and hoped and pray that I would see the rising and falling of her chest as she breathed, but she was not breathing and her chest did not move. My mother was no longer there. She had gone, far away, but I knew she was not alone, for whoever or whatever she saw as she gazed up to the ceiling went with her and I would never know.

My mother, Bernice, was a kind and sensitive woman who was wise, and when not sharing her nuggets of wisdom was a very private person. She also stuck to the rules as she was extremely honest. Whether it was angels, loved ones or something else she saw and experienced as she gazed towards the sky, as she lay in the hospital bed, she kept what she saw to herself. Others have spoken of near-death experiences and the presence of a bright light or loved ones coming to greet them. For me, that was the closest I have ever got to such an experience, through my mother's silent eyes.

The issue of life and death and other spiritual matters are things I have contemplated for the best part of my life, often for different reasons throughout my growing up. As well as having a wonderful mother and father and seven great brothers, I also experienced abuse in childhood at the hands of a friend of the family. Hence, I spent many years wondering why God would allow such a thing to happen to small children. I also experienced great depression and suicidal tendencies. At one point, I feared the idea of never dying, then heard of reincarnation and thought, what if I am reborn only to suffer all over again. I had to learn more about all this if only to ease the fears I had of life and death and to clarify which one I wanted.

I grew up in the Brent area of London with five of my brothers and parents. Mother was an occasional churchgoer until later on in life when she went on a regular basis as she did in childhood. Father would go along as and when he felt like it. As small children we went to Bible class, but that was more about fun, dressing up and seeing friends. It was just a nice break from the house rather than being anything to do with God and the church for us. I did wonder, however, why people spoke of the fear of God. I thought if he created us, why should we fear him, wouldn't it be better to love him. I also did not like the idea of having to go through this middle man Jesus to get to God. Why couldn't I go directly to God, I wondered? At that stage in my life there was very little that I understood. Now I know that going through Jesus to God is simply a matter of being like Jesus and appreciating that Jesus is another aspect of God, if that is how one sees God. I also now know that God is perceived in many different ways and I believe it does not matter which way, just so long as there is a perception of this force or energy that is willing and able to work with us for greater wholeness.

So, there was I, a regular little Black girl, surrounded by a house full of boys, which caused me to feel quite alone at times, as well as the fact that in secret I was trying to deal with this trauma of sexual abuse that I could not understand or talk about. It was also the late 60s, early 70s, and racism was very blatant and commonplace and I could not understand that either, why some people hated other people without even knowing them. I had a lot of unanswered questions and nowhere to turn but within myself. As an adult, I now know that the only place to find true answers is within oneself that takes into account my concept of 'one's self'. This has also changed over the years and at times caused more or less confusion, depending on what I was discovering and how it made me feel. My method of trying to make sense of the world in a situation where I felt I could not speak to others about my fears and fantasies brought me to a place where I would turn to books, seeking answers. Even then I often hid the books I read as they were usually about rape, incest victims or how people think—you know, the stuff about personalities or relationships. The reading thing of course only developed some time after I learnt to read. I had learnt to read late in life at the age of nine. I did not know at the time that I was dyslexic, and that hindered my reading progress and I believe also fuelled my intelligence and skill in finding other ways of discovering things, such as skilfully engaging people in conversations, which allowed them to tell me about a subject I was intrigued with and could talk about openly, like life after death, why people love each other, what is the point of having feelings etc. I learnt a great deal that way and still do. In childhood, I was often referred to as very morbid. My mother would say that I was overdramatic and melancholic, as would my English teacher in secondary school. Yes, I had quite an imagination, and for me the world in my head was often a much safer and more understandable place than the world earthly people dwelled in.

My journey into spiritual awakening began way before I realised it. Not only did I have the most powerful dreams, but as a child I knew there was something more, something elusive and yet tangible. I knew that I was connected to it and that it gave me special powers. Oh, how I wish this was easy to explain, but it consists of so much feeling and inner knowing, that I can hardly find words to describe the unfolding of all that I came to realise. (Please note that I now think we all have these special powers, but many have not discovered how to use them.)

As a child I became quite fixated with older people whom I knew some weeks in advance were going to die, whether they were ill or not. I would pester my mother to allow me to visit them. She often became concerned with my reason for wanting to visit this person, and her protectiveness or procrastination meant on occasion that they would die before I saw them. Then Mum would say, "You knew something, didn't you? I am sorry I did not let you go and visit."

My family were always spiritually aware and accepted that there was something greater at 'work' than us. My mother would often say to me, "What did you dream last night? Anything we need to know?" If my one of my brothers was going for an interview or doing something adventurous or even dangerous, they would ask me to look out for any signs or information in my dreams. On one occasion my brother Winny had an adventure later that week and he had asked me to be aware of any significant insights from my dreams. That week, I dreamt I saw a white van parked by the roadside with a slim black man wearing a colourful shirt. Such a shirt was not really the popular thing at that time for young men from the community, so I figured he was a newcomer and that his actions should not be trusted. I warned my brother that all would be fine unless he saw the man in the colourful shirt near the street curb where a white van was parked. He said he knew the guy who might be wearing such a shirt and he would be aware just in case. I never knew what the situation was that my brother was involved in but he told me that the warning gave him a jump start on a situation that he needed to avoid. This was not a big thing. He just said, 'Yeah sis, your dream was useful, thanks for that," and we left it at that.

Several members of the family and others that I knew in our community had insight regarding matters to come or situations that were about to unfold in their lives. They would receive pre-warnings of potential dangers or deceits planned by others. Then they would silently act on these warnings. We all felt it was very natural, as do many African and Caribbean people. Hence, the Jamaican people say 'one mind told me' something was not right, for example, or that I would see you today or there would be trouble etc. The 'one mind' that the old time saying refers to is that inner voice that is perceived as coming from a different source other than self yet communicating on an inner level to individuals.

Within our house we had a small kitchen. Beyond it was the dining room leading to the back garden. Before the kitchen at the end of the corridor was the stairs and further ahead was the living room, just before the front door. To enter the kitchen from the front door, one would need to pass the living room on the right, take a slight detour where the stairs started and round the bend was the corridor to the kitchen. In other words, you could stand in the kitchen and if you positioned yourself to the far left, you would be able to see the front door.

I remember as a teenager standing just at the entrance of the kitchen looking down the corridor, towards the front door. If I stood sideways and looked through the corner of my eye, just at that point of the hallway where it bent near the stairs, I would see a figure of a short man in a long black or dark grey tailcoat. He was well dressed, had a roundish face and looked very dignified. I would stand there looking at him, then looking away and looking back again. While my mother was busily cooking, I would describe the man to her and ask her who he was. Without interrupting her cooking process or even stopping to look at me, Mum would say, "That sounds like your grandfather, Uncle Andrew (as he was commonly referred to)." Mum would proceed to tell me, "Your grandfather once wore a suit just like that to..." and then I would get a ream of stories about Granddad's violin playing adventures and how everybody respected and honoured him.

Mother was never spooked by the things I saw, but she did not like me saying goodbye to rooms that did not have people in them, which I often did as I felt spiritual presence and knew they were not empty. When I questioned why I should not say goodbye to the 'empty' rooms, she said, "Well, you don't know just who you are talking to, do you?" This was logical but a little selfish, I thought. It was OK to converse with known spirits, but unknowns were not allowed. To me, it was exactly the same thing as mother telling me not to talk to strangers. Left with me was a feeling of how could I get to know anything if I did not branch out and discover the unknown? Mum would say at that point, "Just don't do it." Even to this day, when I say goodbye to an 'empty' room, I remember my mother's warning.

Not all my experiences of connecting with spirit have been sweet and dandy. On one occasion in that very same house in Willesden, London, where I use to see my grandfather, Uncle Andrew, I recall being in my bedroom—a small room at the top of the stairs, back of the house, directly above the dining room. My single bed was situated away from the window, in line with the bedroom door and close up against the wall. It was about 1am in the morning and we had all recently gone to bed. The house in Willesden is a four-bedroom house, which was not much space for a family of five boys, me and my parents. Mum and Dad slept in the big room at the front of the house. My two little brothers had the room beside my parents. I was at the back of the house. My two elder brothers slept in a room downstairs off the corridor that led to the kitchen—their room was situated after the living room and just beyond the stairs. My other brother, Winston, the one born before me, slept in the dining room on a makeshift bed, directly downstairs and below my bedroom. On this particular evening, we had, as usual, chatted, watched TV and slowly drifted off to bed, one by one. Our parents were in bed hours before.

As I settled for the night, I got under the blankets (and it was blankets, not quilts in those days), turned on my left side and curled my knees up to my chin. I was ready to fall asleep, when I heard this deep slow breathing underneath me and I mean directly underneath me as though I was lying on top of someone, so I changed position and lay flat on my stomach. I could still hear this long, slow, deep breathing. Now it sounded softer, like a woman breathing. It was not coarse enough to be a man breathing and it felt so close to me. I held my breath, thinking this must be my own breathing that I could hear. Yet the timely breathing continued. I got up and looked under the bed, because these sounds had to be coming from somewhere, but there was nothing there. I got back into the bed and the breathing still continued.

I wrapped the blankets under my toes and over my head, clutching tightly to as much of it as I could. I curled up into a little ball, wondering what or who this could be. I knew it couldn't be mice as they never made sounds like this. We were very familiar to the sounds of mice over the years. They would scratch, scuttle and squeak, yet usually if you made a bigger or louder sound, they would be silent. Oh, the amount of noise I had already made. I had got out of bed, switched on the light, disrupted chairs to look under the bed. If this breathing sound was coming from underneath the bed, then I was going to find out just what it was, even though I was terrified to look.

Well, I crawled out, turned on the light and took a breath which I held, while I bent over tentatively to look under the bed. There was nothing there. I looked around the room, told myself that it was now OK and went back into bed. As I lay there, I could hear the breathing so very close now that it was right under me, as though the sound was pressed up against my chest, and I was definitely scared—a curious little black girl, all of thirteen years old. Open minded and spiritually accepting I was, but this I could not fathom out. The noises were in my space and I had no control over it.

As I groped through the corners of my mind for a solution whilst struggling to keep at bay the thoughts of what might happen next, I remembered my mother's words about 'don't say goodbye to rooms'. I felt this was my own fault and I had somehow called upon myself something terrible, for which I would now have to suffer the consequences. I knew it would be pointless to run, as now I felt the slow deep rhythmic breathing was attached to my body. Fear had now gripped me, and I was stuck, unable to move, think or defend myself. As I lay there in this numb statue-like state, an irrational but pleasurable thought came to mind. What if, by some chance, this breathing that I was hearing was indeed the breathing of my brother Winston, who slept below me in the dining room downstairs. With this slight glimmer of hope, I felt myself inhale. I got ready to call his name, with all my might. At which point I heard my own name, loud, intense and passionately being called from downstairs. Winston was shouting to me.

I answered him swiftly. "Can you hear it?" he said. I was no longer alone and with great relief I replied, "Yes I can." He came rushing up the stairs and repeated his question with more detail this time. "Can you hear the breathing?" We got into a frenzied dialogue about the breathing. He could hear it directly above him and I heard it directly beneath me. We concluded it must be in the floorboards and therefore not connected to us. We were also relieved to acknowledge that neither of us was going mad, as we both heard it. The one thing we were definitely forbidden to do in our family was to go mad. Other than insanity, most other things that one could do would be accepted on some level within the family. This was an unspoken rule that we all knew. After some time, Winston went back to his room, I relaxed in my bed and we both slept OK that night.

On rising in the morning, we told the family the story of the strange unidentified breathing of the night before and once again we all exchanged other phenomena that had occurred over the years. Some expressed ideas and theories as to why the breathing came, others dismissed it as the creation of our own minds expressed freely in the space between us. Ultimately, we all agreed to accept that there are some things we will never totally know or understand.

Life is full of mysteries. Some may think that such things could never be true. However, if you were to visit places such as Jamaica or Africa, so much would be revealed to you if you had the time to listen and the mind to accept that what we perceive as reality is often only half the story, but remember everyone sees the story differently, there is your perception the other person's perception and the reality, hence we have the trilogy.

# Chapter 8

## What Daddy knew about spirit back home?

Blessed or what, the faint distant voices of little children playing next door, the occasional barking of dogs even further afield, not so far away, two or three birds twittering in the small trees in the long narrow back garden outside the window. Still further, the sound of banging, maybe someone fixing something at the back of their house, or it could be part of the sound of the little children playing. Either way I am so blessed to be able to hear and comprehend the many sounds of life around me.

I watch the cream-leafed patterned curtain gently moving against the open window. Then I become conscious of the trees dancing in the wind to the same tune that the curtains sway. The carpet has been in this tiny little room for as long as I can remember. The ceiling is now a dull yellowish white with little cracks in the corners. As I lie on the single bed that creaks and squeaks at the slightest movement, I am reminded that this little box room in the back of Aunt May's house has been the same ever since I was a little girl. This is the room I would dream in. Here in this tiny box room with a small dressing table, a stool and the single bed, inches away from the window, I would create all sorts of stories and imagine a whole life time of events. For hours and hours, I would just sit there and picture these amazing things and situations in my head. Little did I know that I was indeed creating my future! In the daydreams, I was always happy and prosperous, with very exciting things happening. Then Aunt May would call me for food and I would come down to earth with a bump, only to realise that my life was not as happy as my day dreams.

Many talk of spirituality coming to them through struggle of some sort. I am sure I could claim the same. However, my family has been steeped in spirituality from as far back as Aunt May can remember. Aunt May is tall with deep brown, dark skin and very handsome features, a woman of distinguished refinery. Aunt May was forever telling me and my five brothers of how things used to be back in the old days. As I was the only girl in the family, my parents would send me away from London to stay in Birmingham during the long school holidays for safekeeping, as they both worked and could not watch over us in the day time. I think the real reason was that my brother's friends would come to the house in large numbers—sometimes up to eight visiting friends, or more, would be there at any one time. And my mother wanted to make sure that no one took advantage of her sweet little girl, namely me.

So I was put on the coach from Victoria and met at the other end by Aunt May or her husband Uncle Dave. This was a wonderful experience where I was truly loved and cared for. With all those days and evenings to listen to Aunt May's stories, I learnt a great deal about the history—her history—of spirituality in Jamaica.

My father, the youngest of his siblings, had six brothers and Aunt May was his only sister born to his mother. Paternal Grandfather John had nineteen children in all, the last daughter he had was born when he was 72 years old. Grandfather John Murray was a butcher by trade and Aunt May told me he used to ride a horse, as cars were few and far between in those days and only the richest had them. Granddad John was a gentle but stern man, who respected his wife; but he would not have his male powers questioned or curtailed by anyone. Hence he had several children in the district and each was treated with respect and love. He owned each and every one and on occasion some would visit Miss Katie, Grandad's wife and my grandmother. Miss Katie was a fine-boned woman with pretty, long hair; she was also very strong and feisty. She would work the land as well as any man. Miss Katie ran a tight ship and commanded the respect from all in the community. She spoke of knowing things, without knowing how she knew them, but she trusted what came to her and would issue warnings to her family, from these thoughts that simply just came to her.

I am so sorry she died before I had an opportunity to meet her or know her, as did all my grandparents. They all died by the time I was five years old in Jamaica and I never left England until I was 15 years old.

In those days it was not wise to let others in the district know that one had such abilities, as jealousy and fear of others would make for a hard time if not a persecuted life. All who lived in the community of the bush in St. Ann's, Jamaica, knew who the families were that could use their 'gifts' (the ability to know without knowing) as well as those families or individuals who would use their 'gifts' of insight and influence for personal gain, such as protection or revenge. Some would go further and would use their art of cursing and bewitching as they saw fit.

Aunt May once told me a story of a family who lived in the district. People feared them and would talk about them, behind their backs of course. They would say things like 'be careful of them people, they can do you things' (meaning they have the ability to do evil things to others), or 'watch them close, they have the power'. Some in the community would take it very seriously and avoid any dealings with such people, who would use their abilities for evil, but they would be polite and sociable with them for fear of anger from them. Others would make great efforts to befriend them, in the hope of never being an enemy to them. Aunt May described the household of one such family, who had the power. There were three brothers and a very pretty sister. They lived down the hill in a family home of decent size, in the valley. Their land backed on to Aunt May's family ground, where my grandparents kept their cows and other animals. Once my grandmother had an argument with this family about the fence and animals, who somehow got out through the fence. The family next door dared to accuse my grandmother of theft of one of their cows. Well, grandma was not having anyone disrespect her, so she marched down the hill, as little and petite as she was, and confronted the land owner. She is reported to have said, "Listen, just because you and your family are into this Obeah business, don't you believe I am scared of you, because you can't do anything to me that I can't match, and further more my husband has enough cows, and we have no need to steal yours."

Aunt May remembered the anxiety and worry she felt as her mother picked up her skirt and went down the hill. When Aunt May's father returned from his daily toil, she quickly ran up to him and told him what her mother had done earlier that day. Grandad John just laughed and said, "Don't worry, sweetie, there are few round here as powerful as your mother." Aunt May was left wondering if this comment referred to her mother's standing in the community, or something else, and at the age of 86 years old Aunt May was still unsure.

It was very interesting how Aunt May came to tell me of this family and their ungodly ways. Some months prior to visiting Aunt May, I had been dating a very handsome young man, who to my surprise came from the same district in Jamaica as my father. This was discovered while we were courting and I gleefully spoke to my dad about this strange coincidence. My father, being a rather silent and reserved man, acknowledged what I said and explained that he knew the young man's family, but did not say much more.

I, however, was very passionate young lady and was head over heels in love with this handsome guy. I so wanted to be with him forever, I kept pleading with him for us to get engaged. After about a year, he must have got sick and tired of me pestering him and on my birthday he produced a ring, stating clearly that this was not an engagement ring, just a friendship ring. I accepted. It was a lovely little ring with opal in the middle and some tiny little blue sapphires around the outer circle of the opal. Well, I was thrilled, I didn't care that we were not engaged—my man had finally bought me a ring. I was all of 19 years old and as happy as could be. That evening I had a drink up for my birthday; it was more like an all-night party with hundreds of people. Many friends and family members came round. We ate and drunk and I showed off my nice new ring to all.

In the early hours of the morning, I and a couple of girlfriends crashed out on my bed, totally exhausted. I fell asleep pretty quickly and dreamt that I was in a car, with the two women who shared the bed with me. In the dream, this car crashed over a big hill, and we all came tumbling out of the car. As we tumbled, each and every stone in the ring went flying all over the place and we were desperately looking for the stones, but to no avail. I awoke from the dream, feeling quite distressed, but relieved to discover that I was only dreaming. I took a sigh of relief and turned to my friends, who had recently woken up to tell them about the awful dream. As I looked at the ring on my finger, I noticed that one stone had indeed fallen out of the ring, and we all knew it was there when we went to sleep.

There was a moment of silence. One girl said, "Oh my God, what does it mean?" The other said, "Let's just look for the stone."

I knew in that moment that the dream was significant and the actual loss of the stone just evidenced this. As my girlfriends frantically pulled up the bed sheets to seek the ring stone, I pondered the meaning of the dream and then announced, "They say if you dream of a car that you are not in, then this is not a good dream." The fact that we were in it means it was probably OK to start with, but we were thrown out. Then something is going to go wrong. One friend commented, "Oh Aqualma, that's old wives' tales," but I was sure that the dream meant my relationship was not going to work and that the handsome guy really did not want me.

We could not find the stone, so I spoke to my mother about the dream, in order to ask her what she thought I should do now. She agreed that something was wrong and that I should give the man back the ring and have nothing to do with him. I questioned mother as to whether she thought he was evil or meant to harm me. Please note this man had been, for the past year, absolute sweetness and light. The kind of guy who would always come to my home with an apple or chocolates for my mother. Why he bought them for her and not me, I do not know. Well, after questioning mother on her view of what the dream was trying to tell me, she responded by saying, "I don't know if he is evil or not, but the dream has told you will unfold, so just fix the ring and give it back to the man and end the relationship. The dream has told you that everything has broken up."

I suggested that maybe I should melt down the ring and make it into a cross to ward of any evil. My mother laughed and said, "If you change the shape, the essence will still be the same. Just give it back, so that it is no longer in your possession."

But I liked the ring and I loved the guy so much, this was hard. I told my sweet man of the stone falling out of the ring, but I did not tell him of the dream. He agreed to replace the stone. I then asked him if he thought it was a sign, the stone falling out on the first night he gave it to me. He replied by being very matter of fact and said, "They're little stones and it is not surprising that one fell out. I will fix it." Which he did. I did not have the heart to give it back to him so I kept the ring in the little brown envelope just as the jewellers had placed it, and my mother kept it in her room for safekeeping and so that it was no longer in my possession. I hoped and prayed that the dream really meant nothing and that my handsome man and I would remain happy.

It was but few months later that my loving relationship with Mr Handsome Ring River was about to be painfully shattered. My brother, the one who thinks it's always best to speak your mind, as long as you are telling the truth, came home one evening and told me that he had seen my man leaving a woman's home, in the early hours of the morning and that his friends had told him that my man's car is often parked outside that woman's house. Well, I was shocked and angry at my brother for telling me. Did I really need to know this information? His response was, "Well I am not lying. You can go and see for yourself any morning, I am sure." So I did.

The next day, I got up real early and I waited outside the woman's house and yes indeed, I saw my man leave and get into his car. In that moment my relationship crashed. I was so angry and hurt that I could not speak for several hours. I decided to confront him and promptly pack him in. On speaking with him, he did not deny it, but vowed not to continue his liaison with the woman. However, I left him anyway, mainly because the shame could not be hidden from my family and friends and my big-mouth brother knew, and this brother in particular was sure to tell others—after all it was the truth.

So the dream came to pass, his car played a significant part in crashing our relationship and, just like the ring, our unity no longer had a complete boundary that could hold it together.

I was now very distressed, upset and alone. So I spoke to my father of Mr Handsome's behaviour. Daddy sat upstairs in his bedroom with the television on, but not watching it, as he always did. Daddy is a tall dark strong man of good features. His high forehead and sharp cheek bones gave him a look of prominence, which was complimented by his well-groomed thin moustache. Even though Dad had the features of a ladies' man, this was balanced by his muscular arms and the hard, grey calluses in the palm of his hands, from all the hard work he did as a spring fitter and heavy-duty machinist. As usual he was smoking his pipe and sitting silently, as if in his own little world and quite content with it. Father calmly asked did I give the ring back. I replied no, and mum's got it. Dad then slowly re-lit his pipe and poised himself, with a very serious look on his face and said, "I did not want to tell you this earlier, but now that you and him are 'done', I can tell you. I grew up with his people in Jamaica. One of his aunties was a very pretty girl, but every man in the district was frightened to go near her." Dad promptly added, "I was not afraid and I used to go to the house, so I know what I am talking about. Dem people-a-Obeah people, don't have nothing to do with them, but now that you and him done, I can tell you."

My mouth fell open and all I could think was, how could my father know this information about Handsome's family and not tell me sooner, Jesus! Doesn't he wish me well? However, in spite of the thoughts, I remembered that my father was a very serious man who you would not dare to disrespect, so I said, "Dad, are you serious?" Calmly, in his deep masculine, quiet voice he said, "I could not tell you before. You would not have believed me and you might have thought that I was just trying to mash up your relationship. This information would have only brought you closer to him."

We sat silently for a while and I remembered how I had pranced around the house declaring in a very loud voice, telling anybody who would listen, what a fine handsome man I had and how one day we would be married. My father was absolutely right, he could not have told me earlier, surely I would have rebelled, and in so doing miss the crucial signs of warning that were ultimately revealed to me. My dad and I continued to talk about this man and his family back home. We wondered if they were still involved in this Obeah stuff and just how much Mr Handsome knew about it, if anything – after all, he grew up in England away from his uncle's and grandfather, who seemed to be the main links to the Obeah stuff (which refers to the ancient African and Caribbean spiritual and ritual practice of healing and protecting or even harming) and it could all just be rumours of small-minded people in a small Jamaican district. Dad went on to tell me a story about this family, which could have been the makings of a horrific twilight zone episode.

I sat watching my father's lips as he spoke in this cool, deep monolithic tone, punctuated only by the odd suck on his pipe and the mass of cloud-like smoke that followed. Occasionally, he would stop and think about what he was going to say next, and as he relived the saga in his mind, he would grunt from the pit of his stomach, then make a sigh and shake his head in disgust and disbelief of what he knew to be the truth and was now ready to share with me. It was as though Dad needed to get ready to reveal it or speak it out loud. His face was pensively serious, this wasn't a fun-filled story. This was, in his opinion, something I needed to know.

I listened with great anticipation. My father didn't often talk to me like this, indeed my father hardly ever spoke at the best of times to anyone but mother in the quiet hours of the night. He is a very *silent* man, but not a *quiet* man—with or without words, we could always feel his presence, and would be humble in his midst. So the fact that he was talking to me at such length told me in no uncertain terms that this was real important.

As the story unfolded, the love and desire I once had for my Mr Handsome ring-giving man swiftly evaporated, like droplets of water on an electric cooker. I could feel a cold chill all over my body. My throat dried up, then my stomach felt like a bottomless pit, totally void, with a tinge of immense fear clothing the surrounding walls of my inside. So I stared at my father's precise, slow-moving lips, fearful of hearing what he had to say, yet terrified of missing a word. I needed to know this.

As the story drew near to its conclusion, my mind started to race with a hundred and one different thoughts. What if my sweet handsome guy had done something, anything to me? Thank God I never met more members of his family, or travelled to Jamaica with him. What if he comes back to me, how will I protect myself? Should I even believe any of this, anyway?

But the story was compelling. Dad concluded the story leaving me dumbfounded and degusted with the detail of the story. Then he said, as he raised his head to look directly at me, "This is not something people have told me, this is something I see and know, with my very own eyes." Dad then took a deep long breath, reached for his heavy, silver pipe lighter and attempted to re-light his pipe. He sucked on it three times, making a loud kissing noise. As the flames rose from the tobacco, he expressed, "Talk to your Aunt May about if she knows how dem is. She will tell you."

Some weeks later, I left our family home in London and took a coach trip to Birmingham to visit Aunt May. I told her that Dad had spoken of Mr Handsome and his family back home. I mentioned the pretty sister that Dad spoke of and, without prompting, Aunt May recounted the very same story.

As Aunt May spoke of Obeah, she quickly added that this was not something she believed in, but knew that it could happen. In her view, some will use herbs and other things to conjure up mixtures that may cause harm to others, but many just said they had such powers to bewitch people in order to keep predators and thieves away from their cattle and property.

Aunt May was a woman who spoke with elegance and clear pronunciation. She was confident and sure of herself, and always spoke as though she was trying to teach you something, that you needed to remember, such as how many eggs you should put in a cake and the importance of whipping the mixture until it is fluffy. She would then ask you a question to ensure that you did understand the thing she was trying to teach you. In fact Aunt May was a teacher of sorts. She used to work as the head housekeeper and senior seamstress, which entailed guiding others of less experience on the path of becoming as skilled as she was. In spite all her efforts and coaching, I never mastered the art of good housekeeping, cooking, knitting or baking to the very high standard that Aunt May upheld until her passing. As we sat in her dining room, after a lovely meal which was served on a well laid-out table, Aunt May spoke of Obeah. "All that is happening today, happened from many years back, but is not written for us to read; this means it may be possible for Obeah to exist if you give it power. Some people would tell lies saying that they could do Obeah to stop others from coming to their home and stealing their goods or cattle." She went on to explain, if a young man was to die suddenly in the village, a woman might spread the rumour that she did this using the Obeah power, in order to scare others into staying away from her land and property.

Aunt May, this woman of very hard and high standards and principles, a dedicated Catholic, went on to explain that 'Black heart man' is another name for the Obeah man. In her understanding, she went on to say that neither she nor her family, back then in Jamaica, spent any time fearing or worshipping those who claimed to do Obeah. My father and his sister and all in the family believed that 'who God blessed, no man cursed'. This is a saying I also grew with and we as a family interpreted it to mean that if our belief is with the power of God, that power that is greater than all would protect us always. So we never gave our power away by presuming any other had dominion over us.

So bearing in mind Aunt May's wise and cautious words about the reason why some may make claims to having powers under the banner of Obeah or that of a Black heart man, let us be mindful not to show prejudice or think bad of those who were given or who chose the title of Obeah people, as their reason at that time may have been sound, or maybe they were wrongfully accused and still possibly their intentions were good, in terms of warding off problems and protecting themselves from harm and loss.

In terms of the history of Obeah, it is a traditional spiritual practice which has evolved into a demonised expression of evil-doing, as a result of desperate people turning to the only source that they had control over, their faith and belief in a power greater than the slave master. Obeah came to the Caribbean with the African slaves, but before the oppression of slaves, the practice of Obeah was a more balanced spiritual process, used for the good of the majority and was called upon for healing, thriving, and revealing appropriate paths by those who had the insight and spiritual power to assist others. When slavery came and escape was not possible for the majority, Obeah became a survival tool and the good practice was replaced with methods that could rightly be classed as spiritual weapons against the oppressive and controlling enemy, the slave masters. When Aunt May and Dad were growing up, the slave masters were gone, but the idea of enemies and loss and oppression still remained.

Father's story did not answer any of the suppositions as to why people would turn to Obeah and whether this was done to protect or attack, but just left me with more unanswered questions.

It is now some forty years since my father sat in that old armchair in his bedroom and told me the most horrific story I had ever heard. I will tell you what he said in a minute but first, let me give you an idea of the type of man my father was. Mr Winchester Adolphus Murray, my father was a tall well-built man, slim and muscular, his hands hardened by car springs and welding work over many years of extremely hard labour in the spring fitting factory where he worked. He was always clean shaven and neat in appearance, yet his very dark skin and serious expression, gave that look of a charming rough and ready man. Like Aunt May, he also had high standards, and in addition he had rigid principles and commanded order in his presence. As children growing up around him, we quickly learnt that his rules were not to be broken and his wife was not to be disrespected. Dad's catchphrase was 'don't let me have to talk twice!'

He was a man who meant business, a man of very few words, except for when his bedroom door was closed late in the evening and we as children could hear him laughing and joking with mum. When we were little, on occasion we would stand outside my parent's door and just listen to them chatting away and laughing together. This was fascinating, strange and comforting, because we could hear Dad being who we hardly ever experienced him being, but as soon as we entered the room, and of course we always knocked first, Dad would become quiet again, only speaking if and when he had to do.

So on the day when Dad told me the story, he and I had been in the room all alone, talking away for over half an hour. As I emerged from the room, dazed with all that he had shared with me, Dad's words still rang in my ears: "Just ask your Aunt May." I made my way on automatic pilot along the short corridor, down the two steps, passing my bedroom at the back of the house, then down the steep stair case to the dining room. A few of my brothers were present, sitting and watching TV. They were curious to know what could have taken so long for Dad to say. They wondered if I had done something wrong and was being told off by Dad, or if they had done something wrong and were due to be told off by Daddy. I assured them that none of us were in trouble, and informed them that Dad did talk a lot about something that was totally mind-blowing and so shocking to hear. My brothers were now keen to hear and turned down the TV in readiness to listen, and I needed to share the unbelievable and overwhelming tale, so I told them what Dad had said with his deep, slow, matter-of-fact voice, with that strong uncompromising Jamaican accent. I will now tell you the whole story that you have been waiting to hear.

"One time, when we were young men in Jamaica, me and the Obeah man son, were both apprenticed at a car repair firm. As I had to pass his yard, down the hill on the way to the car repair workshop, I would stop and call for him. Sometimes I would go in and have a cool drink, other times I would meet him at the gate. One fine day I was in his house, waiting for him to get ready, when his big brother said, 'Someone come inna de yard and steal two of mi goat, well this time I am going to set for them.' Me, being a curious young man, I enquired what type of trap he was going to set. He replied, 'I am not talking about any mechanical trap. I mix up sum ting and God help the person who steal mi goat. In the next three days all will be revealed, whether dem steal a next goat or not.'

"Soon after that the younger brother was ready and we left for work. As we was walking down the hill, I asked the younger brother why his big brother is always talking about these Obeah tings and commented that he must think I believe in those things. Little brother said, 'Him, don't underestimate my big brother, he means what he says.'

"Come the Friday evening, three days later, after work, young brother and I pass by his house and I stopped for a drink. We entered the kitchen and the middle brother was there. As he turned around, we got the shock of our lives. His face was distorted. This was a dark skin man, yet all of a sudden, his skin turned a lighter colour and his lips look like they were blown up like a balloon, until they hanged all the way down to his chin. You could hardly see his left eye, due to the fatness and redness of the folding skin. Just as I was about to ask him what happen, he started to talk, explaining that he woke up that morning to feel his face burning him as if it was on fire. He applied cold water and all sorts of natural bush, but nothing worked. The burning just continued. People could not afford to go to the doctor in those days, so you did what you could at home if you became sick. Little brother never said a word, he just stared at him with his mouth wide open and his head hanged low. Well, then big brother walked in and took one look at his brother with the swollen face and turned to put the kettle on the stove, as if nothing had happened.

"I started to talk about the need to find money to go the doctor, as the face condition looked like something that was going to get worse, before it get better. Big brother turn round and say, 'Doctor can't help him.' Then he looked directly at the swollen-face brother and asked him, if you wanted couple of my goat, why didn't you ask me? Without waiting for an answer, he added, 'Dat face is going to swell till it burst and I can't help you now. At that point, I knew it was time to leave, so I didn't bother with the drink, but as I looked at the younger brother, he was now standing with his mouth closed, head held high, his breathing deep and shallow. He stood staring into thin air, with an expressionless look on his face. I just reached out and touched his arm as I passed him and said, 'See you tomorrow.' This was not my business and little brother and I never mentioned it again."

Dad talked then of how that day he took a slow walk up the hill to his home, desperately trying to rid his mind of the horrible image of that distorted face and the reality of how it got like that. Dad took his big sister, Aunt May to one side and quietly told her of what he had just experienced. As young as she was, Aunt May was wise, so she reminded her little brother not to let their mother know that he visited the home down the hill and advised him never to discuss those people's business with anyone.

Having heard the story, the only comment my brothers made was to state that they always thought my ex-boyfriend, Mr Handsome, as I would call him, was always trying too hard to please, so they were not surprised to hear that he came from an Obeah family. I was just pleased that I got out of the relationship when I did.

# Chapter 9

## The Foundation of My Belief and Spiritual Practice.

When I mention to people that I am an interfaith minister, people often ask me first what that means. I explain by telling them that an interfaith minister is someone who has been ordained and is respectful of all religions, spiritual beliefs and practices that honour God in any way or form. Interfaith ministers minister unto those of any faith as long as they value the idea of one God, even if that one God is worshiped in many forms, such as the Shaman practices of worshiping the spirit in nature, trees, water and air with a belief that all universal forces are ultimately connected and can be utilised for the greater good of individuals and the planet, or Hinduism where God is perceived within a multifaceted and diverse set of beliefs, including a wide range of philosophies such as the law of Karma and other views captured in spiritual scriptures such as the Bhagavad Gita and the Upanishads.

I often explain my ministry to those of any religion or spiritual faith in a way that the individual desires—we make it up uniquely according to their wishes. For example, if I am doing a baby blessing, I will design the ceremony with the parent and ask them to consider the impact that they want the Most High to have in the life of their child/children. I will always honour the spiritual belief of the person I am serving, no matter if their belief is very different from mine, as serving the Most High is not about me trying to convince people to believe what I believe or practice

Honouring the Most High in a way that I do. My perspective is that as long as they are working in accordance with the law of the spiritual energy, call it what you like, Yahweh, JAH, God, Buddha or universal force, it's fine with me—because I know there is only one power, one source who is skilled and flexible enough to meet us all, and will communicate with us all no matter what our language or spiritual practice. We are complex beings who function in different ways. This is alright as we have free spirits and free will, hence our blessed mother/father God will accept us, no matter what route we take to get there or what name we choose to use. Have you ever heard of a child being rejected because it calls grandparent, nana or grandma or Baba? No, the grandparent is just pleased that the child is relating to them and calling to them. So it is, in my view, with the Most High.

The practice of accepting others' beliefs as well as those with no beliefs has allowed me to connect with and support many without them feeling judged or questioned regarding their lifestyle. I recall attending a party many years ago. Previous to this I had not known the host of the party, but I heard he had at least one party every year and had been doing so for the past twenty years. This was the Christmas time party. This event had become so well known that invitations were no longer necessary—people would just turn up at the appointed time every year. He held the party in his home and did the cooking himself. People would bring a bottle to help out with the drinks situation and often they would bring a friend. That is how I came to be there. The party had a lovely atmosphere of long-lost friends coming together, but there were so many long-lost friends that space was limited and intimacy of all present was instantly created. People often had to squeeze past each other to move, but all did so in an accepting and respectful way. For some reason, I felt compelled to talk to the host about spirituality and to assist him in utilising his spiritual energy. Now, the party was buzzing with lively conversation and music. Most were singing along too, so this would not be the best time to talk to the host. I therefore introduced myself to him and told him I would like to talk to him about matters of the spirit and asked if I could visit him the next day to have this talk. He looked at me as if he thought I was strange, but said, "Yeah, you can come and talk to me if you want to." I imagine he must have thought that I was skilfully trying to chat him up.

He was definitely attractive and worth any woman's attention, but that was not my motivation, in fact, I do not know quite what motivated me to speak to him and did not think much about it that night. I was far too busy drinking, chatting and partying. The next day, however, I woke and remember thinking I had to fulfil my promise, so I went to visit the host of the party that evening.

He was welcoming and indeed remembered I was coming. Very soon, we were busy talking about his understanding of God and spirituality. He expressed a great deal about his journey to what he now believed and some of the hardship on the way to that belief. We talked of his inner power and his desires. I am sure he would not mind me telling you, he came to a place in his life where he felt that any achievement he would make would be done all alone with no support from any other source. We spoke about the spiritual source within him and how he could call upon this energy to enable him to have greater achievements. In order to maintain confidentiality, let me just say that he took the conversation on board and utilised his inner power to produce greater satisfaction in his life. We have remained good friends and I have been to several of his parties since, and nowadays he refers to me as his spiritual advisor. For me, this is my spiritual path, to be there for others, by taking heed when spirit speaks to me and encourages me to move and impact on the lives of others in a positive way.

I am often asked what I believe. This, for me is a difficult question as my beliefs are very holistic and consist of a lifelong journey to the place I have arrived at today, and indeed I am still exploring and growing spiritually. Before answering this question it would be easier to explain that my beliefs allow me to take on board several different spiritual practices to fulfil my needs. I meditate, and chant and pray and contemplate, and I do this in several different ways. I love the Guyatri mantra which is usually practised by the Hindus. I embrace Egyptian chants as practised by the Ausur Auset society, I learned to drum and sing my prayers via the Rastafarian faith, my Christian upbringing taught me of solemn prayer, silent and otherwise, and I learnt the art of affirming and giving thanks via my teachings of positive thinking and metaphysics. These things I have mentioned are just tips of the iceberg. If I learn a new spiritual practice and it feels good to me, I will incorporate it into my daily or weekly practice. Then again, I adapt some that feel good together, for example, I learnt yoga and found it was great to chant silently while completing my movements. Indeed, even in the gym I chant positive affirmations while exercising vigorously and find this to be a powerful practice.

So let me tell you what I believe. As you now know, I started searching for a spiritual understanding, or rather at that time a religious path, from the age of twelve years old. I walked from church to church, in the hope that I would find something that allowed me to feel comfortable and as though I belonged, something that honoured me as an individual black female, who was intelligent and as worthy as any man. This search went on for years; I tried Pentecostal churches, Baptist churches, the Rasta faith, Buddhism, the Nation of Islam, but none of these were able to hold my interest or satisfy my sense of belonging. Some I felt were sexist, others were controlling and most did not give me a sense of unconditional belonging, which I was yearning for, just to be accepted as I was.

I then discovered the Inter-Faith Seminary. This was a collection of some forty or fifty people who came from many different faiths and beliefs. The purpose of their coming together was to discover more about spirituality, religious beliefs in general and something deeper about themselves and their connection with the thing they perceived as guiding them. I learnt a great deal about different faiths and ritualistic practices, as well as gaining deeper insight into my true self. I studied spiritual counselling and the art of performing weddings, baby blessings, funerals and other types of blessings. On embarking on this journey, I only wanted to discover more about religions and faiths, but I felt so accepted as myself without the need to change that I decided to become ordained as an interfaith minister. This was an amazing experience that has shaped my future existence and experiences. I feel honoured to take part in other people's lives as their minister. I now have children I have blessed who see me as a spiritual aunt and I have people whom I have blessed in marriage who remember me in terms of their commitment to each other. This is a great honour and a blessing in and of itself.

Fundamentally, I believe that we all have the capacity to heal and to be healed. It is my view that God works through us in many different ways, whether we know it or not. I think we are born with a very loose script that has several paths woven throughout it that may bring us to the place where we can fulfil our purpose. However, we have within us the power and authority to change the script, for better or for worse. The choices, achievements and consequences are ultimately ours, once we are mature enough to take appropriate action and responsibility. I believe all the spiritual books such as the Bible, Quran and others have a message that can assist and guide us.

Spiritually, I think of myself as a medium and clairvoyant, with the gift of communicating with past souls and energies within the universe. I pray that such connections with spirit and energy are all good and positive and I trust that my prayers are answered as I have free will and the inner authority to create in my life just what I desire.

**An alternative image of chakras by my Nieces Io-May Murray and Ola Bernice Murray**

A Blissful view from my Garden, reminding me of nature, animals and the beauty of our planet Earth. Sometimes we see what we want to see and other times we can see the branches of the tree, the bird and the cat.

# Chapter 10

## What is Spirituality?

Spirituality is knowing that you are in the same place as God all the time. I am not just talking about those of us who have taken up religion, but all of us. The reality is, you see, we need do nothing but know and acknowledge the reality of God. Then God acknowledges us. It's like going to a party and standing in a dark corner. No one would remember that you were there, but if you were to go up to a few people and say hi my name is... then some would remember you were there.

Spirituality is really knowing that you are spirit and that spirit is you. Today I gave a reading to_a man who said, "Ask him his name so that I know it is him for sure." The spirit communicating with me just laughed and mentioned an experience that was had on the earth plane as a way of identifying himself. Why did the spirit not give me his name? Well, spirit does not work like that. I have come to discover that the only place where names are important is on the earth plane. Beyond this life there are no such things as individual entities, everything is infinitely connected and is aware of all its parts and its wholeness, and hence there is no need for separate names. I feel this is also true of our Lord the Most High, so some call him Jah, others say Jesus, while some say Elohim and more say God—either way, we are still talking about the one God, the universal force the energy and the light that guides and protects us.

When spirits are asked for names they just laugh unless they are still deeply connected to the earth plane. Asking spirit for a name is a bit like asking somebody, "When was the first time you ate ice cream?" The question is no longer relevant or important. What's important is knowing that you had the experience for better or for worse.

As a medium I often get names of people, but I tend to find that those people are still on the earth plane. I am gifted insomuch that I find I can often speak to the spirit of those who are still on the earth plane. Indeed, sometimes I find it hard to tell the difference between those who have passed on and those who are still living. This amazes me as it simply proves that we are so connected and not so different.

I believe firmly that if we align ourselves with God, we open the channels to so many wonderful experiences in a safe and comfortable way. How might one connect or become aligned with God? I would say through perceiving the Most High as the only truth and trusting this source to bring you only good experiences and situations. It boils down to TRUST. For me, trust means 'To React Unconditionally Supported by Truth'. Another way of expressing the oneness and love of God is to see the word trust as representing 'Together, Respecting, Unified, Sustained, Truth' (TRUST).

The concept of God being truth is hard for some to understand. Truth does not necessarily mean right or appropriate but talks more of the fundamental essence of something. The idea of truth describes what is left when one removes ego, motivation, selfish expectations and desires. Truth is genuine acceptance, motiveless giving and pure intentions. Jesus talked of being the way, the truth and the light. I interpret those words as meaning 'I am the path of absolute love that will ultimately bring you joy and peace'. Imagine how extraordinary, how wonderful, safe and comfortable it must feel to TRUST in the TRUTH of GOD, (most high, or universal force).

# Chapter 11

# W.I.S.D.O.M (Whole Inner Spiritual Development of Me)

The word 'wisdom' has come to mean knowledge gained over a long period of time by an astute and intelligent person who has learned when and when not to express it. Wisdom is often perceived as the gift given to those who have extensive life experiences and/or years. The faculty defined as wisdom pertains to information, insight and clarity regarding particular issues or theoretical understanding of situations in general or specifically, i.e., 'the wise old man knew it was better to walk downhill to sell his load of goods than uphill'. (For the simple reason that it is easier to bring a heavy load downhill than up and the thought of returning home without selling all the goods meant that a heavy load would result in a struggle to return them home on uphill terrain, hence the old man had more of an incentive to sell as much of his goods as possible and more energy in which to achieve this task, as he had taken the easier and less strenuous route to his selling destination.)

The *Collins Pocket English Dictionary* defines the word 'wisdom' as meaning '1. The quality of being wise. 2. Learning; Knowledge. ...' (976: 1981). The explanation of the word 'wisdom' places the insight and learning from an outside source that requires internalising and appropriate application.

From a spiritual perspective, the word 'wisdom' has a totally different meaning, but this is rarely understood or acknowledged. Many individuals will talk about their growing wisdom as they gather more information and understanding from books or workshops; hence, they are referring to the dictionary's interpretation of the meaning behind the word 'wisdom'. Some people will make reference to the idea of inner wisdom as a separate and different kind of wisdom than the common use of the word. This, in my view, is a distortion of the reality of what wisdom really is.

The acronym used at the beginning of this chapter captures the true essence of the word wisdom. In my opinion, wisdom sits in the very centre of our soul. It is that wealth of knowledge, insight and information which we are all blessed with, indeed it is the store house of God. As we build our unity with the Most High, we have more and more access to this inner wisdom. It is a bit like a child learning to read. At first it is hard work and the words and rules of meaning make little sense. Once the concept of reading is grasped, one forgets the struggle and finds that most words can be translated into something that has meaning and is understood by the individual.

Spiritual literacy acts on the same principle but is slightly different in experience. The more you discover about spirituality, the less you think you know. Now why is that? Some would say that all we think we know on the earthly plain is but an illusion and far from the reality of existence and being. Hence, when spirituality unfolds, we have to unlearn a lot of preconceived idea which our spiritual experiences have proven to be false. Let me attempt to explain. At the age of twenty-one I went to visit family in Canada. I had just had my baby boy six months earlier and needed a break. My mother and father agreed to care for the baby in my absence. My aunt lived in a lovely big house with her two children and my cousin's girlfriend. My mother's sister was very accepting of me and the family did all they could to make me comfortable. I partied, toured and had a lot of fun. One night as a slept in my auntie's bed, I dreamt that I was dying. I stood inside a building I did not know, before a small square window. Beside me stood this very strong eunuch type man with olive-coloured skin, big biceps and no expression on his face. I could feel myself becoming weaker and weaker and as I slipped to the ground he would gently raise me up so that I could see out of the window. I noticed that in the view from the window, I could see a number of friends and family members walking by. The associates and family members did not notice me, but as they passed I said goodbye to them from my small strange room, through the little window. I then felt the energy leaving my body and I could not say goodbye anymore. At this point, however, I felt I had said goodbye to everybody. The strong olive-skinned man was about to lead me away from the window when I noticed a friend, Wayne, passing by and I knew I did not have the energy to bid him farewell. I felt sad and guilty for not saying goodbye to him and started to cry in the dream, at which point I woke up.

I woke up feeling quite confused and a little scared as I really thought I was dying. On telling my aunt about the dream, she said, "Well, dreams of death usually mean marriage, but you didn't die did you?" "No," I replied. "I was just dying."

After a few more days of fun in the hot city of Toronto, I returned home to my baby and the grey cloudy skies of London which I was very pleased to see. I was even more pleased to still be alive. Finally, I had an opportunity to sit and relax in my very own front room. I sat next to the dressing table which backed onto the bay windows in my bedroom and went through the small collection of post that had arrived in the past ten days. As you would expect, there were several bills amongst the post, some junk mail and a letter of invitation. I opened the pretty cream invitation envelope to find a dainty card inviting me to the engagement party of Wayne and his partner. I knew instantly that Wayne would never marry this girl, as I had not had the opportunity to say goodbye to him in the dream. Of course, I never told him this. It did not feel appropriate to do so. I told my mother and brothers of the dream and my interpretation, and as usual they said, "Um, it's possible."

The engagement party was great and all had a wonderful time. The young lovers seemed very happy, so I simply wished them the best and hoped that they would learn relevant lessons from their current experience and find suitable love in others rather than each other, in the long run.

Six months later, the romance was over and they had parted. This came as no surprise to me, even though others were very shocked. Many years on, Wayne has a new partner and several wonderful children. He is a committed and dedicated father and for all intents and purposes appears very happy with his common law wife. Maybe one day, if the situation should arise, I will tell him of the dream. Somewhere in this universe the outcome of Wayne's relationship with his fiancée was known to others and revealed to me in the dream. I believe this knowledge comes from the pit of our soul where God resides. But what was the purpose of revealing this to me? Well, I suppose I would have to grasp the vast depth of the bigger picture to answer this question in all honesty, but from my place of relative ignorance regarding spiritual matters, let me take a guess. I think sometimes we are shown things that are not logical or rational for us to know as an example of the greater force working from within us, the God power opening up to us, in preparation for the greater things that would be revealed to us. In truth, I had a schoolgirl crush on Wayne, and we had since become good friends, which made him a very significant person to me and by the very fact that I was dying in the dream that was quite dramatic to experience, even in a dream. This ensured that I would more than likely remember that dream for years to come, as I did. The interpretation of the dream, however. Was the blessing passed down to me via the Most High, through the ancestry? I think the purpose of this dream being revealed to me and the subsequent outcome was the Lord's way of saying, "I want to communicate with you and reveal many things to you. If you would just listen and acknowledge my presence within the depths of your soul. There is work for us to do and I need you to hear me."

This was a great strategy by the Most High—what better way to get the attention of a young spiritually minded girl? It worked. I started trusting my dreams more and my ability to interpret them. I was keen to explore my spirituality and discover just what God meant to me as well as others. I know that I am not special and that the Lord is attempting to communicate with us all, if only we would not dismiss what seems illogical and embrace the reality of this wisdom called God or the Most High or universal force, which sits in the depths of each and everyone's soul.

Deep inside me, I know that there is a cause for all that happens to each of us. Sometimes this is hard to grasp, especially when horrible things happen to us. But I have learnt to ask myself where is the gem in that experience, what is it that I need to be learning? Today I pray: 'Dear Lord bring me your lessons without the pain. I am ready to grasp your wisdom.'

I have heard it said that many who find their way to God have come there from a place of suffering, from life experience. I believe this is true. I don't believe, however, that we all need to suffer to find God. If only someone would explain to us just what we need to do to find God painlessly,

I am sure this would alleviate many of the experiences of suffering that bring us close to God. My mother had a saying that she would tell my brothers and me when we had disobeyed her or not followed an instruction quickly enough. It was 'If you can't hear, then you must feel'. As a girl, I presumed that meant that if we did not do as we were told, she would smack us or punish us in some other way and we would therefore become acutely aware of the consequences of our (irresponsible?) non-actions. As an adult, I fully comprehend the true meanings of her words. What mum was really trying to tell us was that we are all guided and supported by a loved one and if we fail to take heed of the lessons through this guidance, then we will suffer the pitfalls that we were being warned against. God is so similar to our parents or loved ones and we so often misunderstand them or ignore them when they are trying to give us guidance and support. On occasion we become so aware of what we should be doing and what would be the right action in a given situation, but for reasons of insecurity, feelings of worthlessness and lack of confidence, we fail to take the correct action, which leaves us open to the negative consequences of not taking heed of the good advice of loved ones or the inner voice of God that was trying to steer us in the right direction.

Others have been reported to say that God whispers to you gently (the 'still small voice') and if you fail to listen, then he raises his voice and may even push you fiercely. Let me give you an example of what I mean. For many years I resented paying bills, mainly because I perceived the prices as extortionate and I could not see the benefits for me in spending all this money, i.e., the council tax, or water rates. I also held a belief that I did not have enough, so I would delay paying bills until the last minute. I also had a pretty low sense of self-value, which caused me to ignore the details of my income or my financial affairs. I was sure that if I contacted the bank, they would only tell me I did not have enough, and that would only make me feel worse, so I often did nothing until the final red letter arrived or the bank charges were piling up. You can imagine the mess I got into. This went on for years. I was comforted, however, with the fact that I had a good job and regular money coming in. Sometimes I would earn extra when I did some training. Even though I knew I would never starve, I worried so much about money. Due to my sense of worthlessness, I would spend large amounts of money on presents for others, but I found it hard to buy myself a new pair of shoes that I desperately needed, and this went on for even more years.

One day, I woke up bright and early and got ready to attend my class at the New Seminary, where I was learning to become an interfaith minister. Before leaving the house, I checked the post. There was a letter from the loan company that had given me the money to buy my leather chairs. I owed them six thousand pounds and the debt was secured against my property. My lovely little three-bedroom house that I had lived in for some eight years. I looked at the letter and noted that they were going to take me to court in order to repossess my home. I closed the envelope and said, "Dear Lord, what is the lesson you are trying to teach me? Help me to learn it quickly so that I do not have to suffer and/or lose my home." I trusted the Lord would reveal the lesson to me before it was too late. Without another thought I set off on my journey to the course.

By the afternoon of that same day, I became extremely distressed and cried uncontrollably. All of a sudden I felt scared, alone, vulnerable and more than anything else, I felt ashamed of my failings to pay my bills. I wondered who I could go to for help and could not think of anyone. All the people close to me usually came to me for help. I wondered why the Lord would allow me to lose the only shelter I had access to. And then there was my teenage son, who would also be without a home. In one instant swoop, my world was crumbling and my faith and trust in God was being seriously tested. Somewhere deep inside I knew the Lord would not leave me without support, but I was just so unsure about my ability to manage the suffering I imagined was about to come. In my mind I did not know where to turn to and I could not hear my inner-God-voice whispering to me so I wept.

I found myself no longer able to contain these feelings alone, so I spoke to the course leader, Miranda Holden, who was kind enough to pray with me, comforted me and held me. Then she suggested something that I found totally terrifying. She said, "You could ask members of this interfaith seminary to help you, I am sure they would be willing." Well, I was shocked and amazed. I responded by saying that no, I could not do that, the shame and embarrassment would kill me. All this was coming from a place of the superwoman syndrome, of course—you know the script. The 'I help myself' script: I need nobody else, I am independent, strong and rely on no man, woman or child for my survival. Well, Miranda simply said, "It's up to you."

Later that day another member of the group became aware of my constant sobbing as I sat trying my best to be attentive to the subject that we were exploring that day. In the break, he put his arms around me and rested my head on his chest, at which point I cried uncontrollably once again. He never questioned me or said 'there. there' or anything. He just held me and I felt so safe and contained.

Subsequently, I spoke to the larger group of the seminary course and explained my distress and shame. They were overwhelmingly supportive and offered all kinds of assistance. One offered large sums of money for as long as I needed it, others offered space in their homes, still others offered legal advice, etc. I couldn't believe the help people were willing to give. I found myself struggling to accept their help—this was not a place I was used to being in. After all, superwoman does not get much experience in accepting help. I felt uncomfortable, awkward, and most definitely humbled by the love and generosity of this group of people whom I had not even known for a year yet.

The weeks following proved to be very stressful. I went to work and broke down in tears again. Again, I found generous and supportive people who were willing to offer me help. The banks and high street building societies were not so generous. Day after day I sat around in such places seeking a loan. But my previous bad credit record and large debts hindered the process. While all this was going on, time was running out and the court date for repossession was looming close.

My son, however, greeted this news with a different attitude than me. He said, after laughing out loud, "This is so exciting—imagine what might happen next!" I promptly asked him, in an angry and disappointed tone, if he realised the gravity and seriousness of the situation. "But mum, can't you see the opportunities that this might bring?" Unable to appreciate his insight and wisdom, I stormed off, to continue filling in more loan forms.

After two weeks of begging and grovelling to banks, only to be rejected time and time again, I gave up and decided to accept my fate whatever it might be. Comforted by the fact that there were some people who would give me a space in their home for a while, and if the worst came to the worst I would not starve. I prayed, "Dear God, it's up to you now. I can do nothing more. Help me to cope with whatever happens next."

I still kept questioning what the spiritual lesson that I needed to be learning here was. By now, I had grasped the fact that it is important that I keep my financial affairs in order and that unless I take some action towards that God is not in a position to help me. Hence, another old saying is evidenced: 'God helps those who help themselves' and, of course, those who can't help themselves. It's a paradox but true. The innocent and the unable are given what they need. Those who have the capacity to use their free will are expected to do so, and the consequences or reaction they receive will be in relation to how they have used or not used their free will. Regarding my financial difficulties, it's my view that I failed to use my free will constructively and suffered the consequences for that. But my God is a merciful and loving God so let me tell you what happened next.

I had been attending a centre outside of London, where I offered training occasionally to their new staff. During my two weeks of distress, I visited this centre and did a day's training with them. On this occasion, I was told that they would be expanding their service and wished to employ more managers. They told me my skills would be greatly appreciated and encouraged me to apply for one of the posts. Accepting such a post would entail moving out of London and leaving my home. As by now I was pretty sure that I was going to lose my home, I thought it would not be such a bad idea. Indeed, I could sell my home and buy a cheaper one outside of London. I agreed. They were keen to have me in post, so interviewed me very quickly and, after I secured the position, they offered me a resettlement package, which meant they would give me somewhere to live until I was able to move. By this stage in the game I was too depressed to get excited about this. However, I was pleased that at least I had an option now. The move would also mean a rise in salary and another opportunity to get my money affairs in order.

I looked around my home where I had lived for eight years. It was the only home I had ever bought. I recalled a number of nostalgic memories, some good, and some bad. I recalled the spiritual cleansing of the house and how I had prayed that it would bring joy and happiness to all who entered. I thought about moving away from my friends and family but was relieved that I now had a good reason to go rather than having to leave my home due to repossession.

The next day, I received a phone call from a friend who I often meditate with. She had dreamt that I was standing in a bright white light, looking so very happy and excited. While in the dream, I was jumping for joy, saying it's great, I have a second mortgage. I said to her, "That's an interesting dream. Are you sure I was not pleased at getting a *re-mortgage*?"—which is what I had been seeking and writing to lenders about. She was adamant. "No, it was most definitely a second mortgage." I thanked her for having such a hopeful dream about me and told her my situation, which she had not previously known about. After all, I was too embarrassed and ashamed to tell many people about my predicament. Like a good spiritual sister, she said, "Well I am sure the Lord has a plan for you, the dream was so clear." I thanked her and thought to myself she must be dreaming about the next home I am going to buy, but that would be a new mortgage not a second mortgage. I very quickly put her dream aside and went on with my busy day at work.

Two days later, with two weeks to go before the repossession court case, whilst in a shopping centre, I received a phone call. "Hello, Miss Murray, are you still interested in re-mortgaging your home. It was obviously one of these many freelance mortgage brokers I had filled out forms for and written to requesting assistance from, in order to save my home. I continued gathering my shopping goods from the shelves and discreetly said, "No thank you, I have decided to sell and move out of London."

The voice at the other end of the phone said, "That's not a wise thing to do; we could re-mortgage your existing property and give you a second mortgage for the property outside of London." I was not quite sure that I heard him correctly, through the hustle and bustle of the store, but the words *second mortgage* stuck in my mind. I stopped and put my shopping basket down and remembered the dream of my spiritual sister.

Having asked for clarification from the voice at the end of the phone, I agreed to meet the mortgage broker within the next few days. Suddenly, I felt extremely light within myself and a little apprehensive. I now knew the dream of my friend was a sign to take this offer seriously no matter what my logical and resistant mind said about the cost. This was one occasion when I needed to put my worthless and low self-values aside and give myself this opportunity. I felt like God had forgiven me for past failings and offered me a second chance. When the broker came round and told me just how much it would all cost (and indeed it was very expensive) I just said yes, yes, yes and signed on the dotted line. I then prayed, "Dear God, you have given me this opportunity for reasons I am not sure of. Please provide me with the money, skills and ability to make it work out for the greater good of all." I decided to trust that God had plan for me and if I worked with Him I would prosper.

Inside of three months, I have purchased a seven-bedroom property outside of London, some six minutes from the new workplace. The new house provides space for a meditation room and study. The garden is beautiful and big with three garden sheds. I now have a real open fire and a long front drive with garage space. The property in London is rented out, which covers the mortgage and gives me a small profit. My salary covers all my expenditures and my lifestyle is so much cheaper. I believe I am truly blessed.

I think there were several spiritual lessons in this situation which I will elaborate on briefly. First and foremost, I suspect the Lord has a plan for me and this new home. Maybe now that I have space, I should run more workshops about positive thinking or spirituality. Maybe I should develop my practice as a medium. The experience might have been about creating an atmosphere and circumstances conducive to completing this very book that you are reading today. Or maybe I should just relax in this comfortable new space and thank God for such luxury. The truth is, if we do not listen to the whispers of the Most High, we will surely be forced to hear, and in the process may feel some distress.

The lessons in the experience of my house and home drama are manifold. The first relates to the need to let go and let God. It is not until we are able to surrender wholeheartedly, either because we are skilled at doing so or because we must, that the Most High is able to step in and offer the support and grace that we so desperately want and often need. Letting go is usually experienced when we have tried so hard and can literally do no more. Imagine how much better and easier it would be if we could only put the energy into trying to let God in and trusting that this is enough, so that we can relax into the letting go. How do we do this? By attempting to remember the Most High as often as we can throughout our waking hours and in your sleep if you can do it. That's about going to bed with God in mind and waking up with God as your first thought. We also need to trust God with the little things in our lives so that we gain an experience of His miracles in our lives. Hence, when the big things come, we can trust in a history of His previous successes and achievements in our lives. This practice will keep you aligned with God and ultimately in His/Her Grace.

A fundamental lesson that was revealed to me in the aforementioned drama is the need to keep our practical and financial affairs in a neat and tidy order. This enables us to spend less time and energy worrying and fretting about mundane things, which ultimately frees us up to focus on higher matters. Keeping our worldly lives in order also gives a clear message to the laws of the universe that we are able to respect and value rules processes and methods. I am sure you have heard the saying 'God gives no one any more than they can handle'. Well, how is God to know what you can handle or rather are prepared to handle save by how you handle the practical and emotional manifestations in your life. Without a doubt, God knows that, given the right guidance and support with the co-operation of your free will, you can handle any and everything that might come your way, if you are willing to let God work with you and for you on occasions.

One of the hardest lessons was learning how to allow my fellow man and woman to help me. I needed to accept that I do not live in vacuum and that interaction with others is not only about being useful to them but also receiving from them. The Blessed One offers support through many different channels, and to reject the assistance of another is indeed to reject God's manifestation of help and support. Learn to receive, knowing that God is the source that fuels all good actions.

The power of asking was also highlighted. Many of us would have had childhood experiences of being too scared to ask or so used to rejection that we stopped asking. As a result, we become so stuck in our past patterns that we may well be praying and asking God to help, but this may be done with an expectation that we won't get what we ask for. In order to break this pattern, we need to ask of those around us enough times to be able to receive. When we see that other people may be willing to give to us we learn to trust that God may also give to us. We are but humans at this time, and it is hard to constantly believe that a God we cannot always feel and know will always give us what we want. If we, however, ask of each other and get what we ask for sometimes, we discover that our peers can meet our needs on occasions. There is the teaching—if man can achieve the task of giving what we ask of him sometimes, then surely we can begin to trust that God has the ability to give us what we ask for every time.

This experience of nearly losing all that I had and all my security nets taught me, in no uncertain terms, that I was not alone. It reminded me that I was not worthless or of no value. I was forced to acknowledge that some people, indeed a great number of people, really care about me. I discovered that I mattered not only to my friends and companions on this earth plane, but also to my God. You can be sure that if I matter, you matter too, since in the eyes of our Father, the Most High we are all one.

Sometimes when nights are lonely and days are long and stressful, it's hard to remember the wholeness of the Most High. The minute we let go of loving ourselves, we allow unloving feelings in, and because we have spent so much time and energy in an unloving state, we manifest negativity in our lives very quickly and easily. It turns up in the form of threats from debt collectors, unreasonable demands from friends, family and employers, and even road rage from strangers.

Our inner being needs to be constantly clothed in our appreciation of ourselves. It's easier when there are people around you to appreciate you. The love you show to them or feel from them is reflected back to you. When we are alone and only have ourselves, then *we* need to be the light that shines back on our inner selves. How do we do this? I hear you asking, when you hardly have time to stop and think, much less to feel love for self. Have you ever wondered why you smile when someone says 'Cheer up, Jesus loves you'? They have gently reminded you that you are not alone and you do have a loving light shining on you at all times. You are truly blessed, even in the loneliest of moments.

When we are feeling pain on an emotional level, it is often very difficult to know what that pain actually feels like, as we are usually so busy experiencing our reaction to the pain. If our heart is broken, we think about what we have lost and what we will never have again, rather than what we are actually feeling. When money is our problem we think about the lack of security and the shame of poverty rather than the reality of emptiness. When we fail at a task or an exam, we resent the work we have put in and fantasise about the humiliation we have brought upon ourselves.

Within all of these reactions, we have denied ourselves the experience of feeling the pain deep down inside us. We prevent ourselves from feeling the real pain for very good reasons, for to feel the pain and know the pain may bring us into a position of comforting ourselves and that would require us to love ourselves. So, what do we do instead? We talk to a friend, therapist or loved one about how dreadful things are. They hear our words and, unlike us, they feel our pain and are encouraged to comfort us. In this way, we reflect their love into the deepest part of us, but because it is not connecting to our feeling of pain, just our words of pain, the relief is not long-lived. It is important to know our pain, sooth our pain and heal our pain within ourselves in order to achieve long-lasting effects.

Through the power of clairvoyance I have had the pleasure and discomfort of experiencing the depths of others' pains. I have had insight into that place where there are no words or boundaries to that vast heavy unexplainable feeling of hurt. What I have learnt from being in that place of others' pains is that while I am feeling with them the reality of their pain, the reason for it becomes irrelevant, the length of time it has been there is irrelevant. The only significant factor in that experience of distress, despair and hurt is that *pain* is taking up the space of *love*. I experience a sense of this person not being filled with love and knowledge of the struggle to find a road back to love. But what really saddens me when I experience this through clairvoyance is that the road to resolving pain and finding love is cluttered with emotions and thoughts of guilt, shame, humiliation and loss. And without the grace of God's unconditional love, I would feel powerless to do anything for them, or hold any hope that they could do it for themselves. Believe me, even though I only feel their pain for a short time, it is a horrendous place to be and I know that for them it is even worse than I have insight into. While I am there, connected with them through the power of God's gift, I let the angels work through me to start the process of clearing the clutter of negative thought and emotions, in order for the light of love to shine through—in the hope that this will encourage the individual to begin the process of comforting themselves and opening the way for love of self. Many people describe a sense of feeling better, no matter what the reading reveals. Some would argue that a person seeking clairvoyance feels better because they have been listened to or that the clairvoyant has offered a time of support and hope for them. None of these things would be wrong. But I would argue that there is another ingredient of an invisible nature that offers the seeker the experience of pure unconditional love—and there is nothing more attractive and powerful than genuine love, which comes directly from the Most High. It is for this reason that people seek readings time and time again.

This situation of receiving God's love directly can be just as easily achieved without words if one is prepared to sit in the silent space while the other allows their form to be used as a channel for God's love. Indeed, many do this already in group meditation or joint prayers and, of course, long silent walks. All these pursuits have the potential for leaving those involved with a sense of receiving connectedness and relief from the place of pain.

The other side to the gifts that clairvoyance brings is that I get to experience the love and warmth that people feel. I recall giving this woman a reading. She was a beautiful Black woman, tall and well proportioned, she had big eyes and full flat lips. Her clothes said very clearly 'I am an organised woman, who knows what she likes to wear'. She was very nervous about the reading, almost as though she was not sure where or how to fit this experience into her life plan. We sat and I took her hands and explained the process to her. Quite soon after, information started to flow and then I felt this very strong feeling of care, passion and desire. I expressed this to her and explained that I could not see anything at this time but could just feel overwhelming love. As I sat with these very nice feelings, a picture started to emerge. I could see the body of a tall man. Well, I could see his chest and shoulders. I explained that I had a man before me with a fine-looking body, who was giving lots of loving feelings, but he was holding back. He seemed shy or maybe reluctant to express all that he felt. I then became aware of some of his personality traits and the work he did. But while all these practical things were coming through, I was still experiencing the intense love he was giving off.

Suddenly, the loving feeling was heightened by a strong, sensitive, sexual energy. Now I could see his arms holding her and touching her in a particular way. She explained that this was her current partner and evidenced that he did indeed touch her in the particular ways that I described. The feeling felt so great, I just had to keep telling her, "He is a lovely man with a great deal to give, but he seems to be holding back." She explained that she found it hard to know quite how he felt as he did not express himself verbally. I was shocked and wondered how she could not feel the love this man was pouring out to her.

Well, when I repeated that this man was so sweet and his love felt so good, she said, in a very abrupt and angry tone (keeping her voice low of course, because she was too lady-like to raise it), "OK that's enough now, stop focusing on my man."

Never before had I experienced someone reacting with such jealousy and fear of loss, which is what possessiveness is. I realised in that moment why this man had been so careful not to express all that he felt for her. Some part of him realised that she might have felt overwhelmed by this or maybe she would fear that his enormous love would somehow annihilate the love she had for herself. It is my theory that she might have grown so used to her inner pain and hurt that it would be most disruptive to her sense of self, as a person separate from others and alone, to have someone pour the light of love into that inner place within her which was so busy coping with the chaos that pain brings.

I attempted to enable her to see that this man's love was a good thing that she could try to let into her heart. From her reaction to this, I fear she was not ready for this message at this time so I simply let go of talking and explaining and just allowed God to work in the hope that God's shining light of love would make way for her partner's love. We rounded off the session by me listening to her talking for some twenty minutes. She found this aspect of the session far more comfortable and we ended amicably. Readings are amazing things and maybe, one day, she will find the gem in that life experience.

# Chapter 12

## Spiritual Empowerment, Inner Power (Read and just imagine. It may change your life.)

The beauty of spirituality is its ability to bring people home to themselves through assisting them in unfolding aspects of themselves that have always been there to help them find the ultimate power within.

This inner force is, in fact, the only power the individual really has and is the only power that they can utilise to enhance or change their lives. All other methods are futile and short-lived because they are, in fact, not real power. Let's take, for example, a young man who is the leader of a well-known and formidable gang. The type of young person who has 'street cred' dresses a certain way that fits in with those who give respect for certain styles and fashion. He has a hairstyle that makes a public statement to those who are in the know, he has the 'backative'. This is a term used amongst young black people as well as street wise youths of all cultures. It signifies support and means that one's back is covered by others who may have power and are willing to assist, many in the community who are feared and looked up to. Hence, others who come across him may allow him to take some control, or wield some decision-making ability or worse may even give over their sense of power to him out of intimidation, hopes of gaining access to the gang's power, or simply in accordance with the street cred rules.

Such a young man may feel powerful within himself to a degree, but there is a part of him that knows that this power is really tentative and could be lost at any time and in so many ways. To lose this power all that would need to happen would be that the majority of the gang decide that another person is more suited to the leadership role. His perceived sense of power could be shattered in a blink of an eye if his style and actions no longer bring them the benefits they signed up to.

I grew up amongst a group of young men who were involved in some criminal activity and community territorial belonging. In those days they would refer to themselves as belonging to a certain 'firm'. On occasion different firms would unite to battle with others who may have threatened their patch of criminal activity and at other times one group might have upset a lead member of another group. Many of the divisions were turf war such as south verses north or black verses white. The 1970's was a very different time when racism was rife, yet young criminals united with different races if and when it suited their greater need, which was usually some criminal activity. I was a young girl growing up around five teenage brothers and all of their friends. They attempted to protect me from most of the details of what was happening, but I knew the fear they engendered and the power and control that my brothers and their friends had in the community we lived in. This caused me to have to be vigilant, cautious and careful when I ventured out, as it was hard to know who might have favoured the firms my brothers associated with or who was angry with them and might want to take their revenge out on me. I kept myself to myself within my community. To this day many people say to me 'Wow we never knew the Murrays had a sister'. I was protected by my brothers as they knew that notoriety could bring powerful benefits as well as shocking consequences.

Perceived power manifests itself in other walks of life as well. Let's take the high-powered executive. They probably work for a big successful firm and have a style of dress that mirrors others who see themselves as high-powered bosses. This usually consists of fitted outer garments, with plain, sober colours, dark shoes and a hair style that is consistent with the latest fashion that can be observed in the top magazines or on media stars who are admired at the time. This is true of nearly all executives, no matter what ethnic background they are identified with. Some will be able to call themselves experts in their field and may have great understanding and experience of their chosen business, just like the aforementioned gang leader. The power that the executive has is based on the current success of their chosen marketplace, and the ability they have to dominate others in that marketplace, again just like the gang leader. But what if the tables should turn and some new product or school of thought shifts them from this position of perceived power? What if others no longer value their service and are unwilling to make use of them. How useful is that level of perceived power? You see, the important thing about real power is the ability for it to be forever consistent and always useful to self and others.

We humans are always doing our best to skilfully manipulate the consistent and self-pervading power that we encounter, e.g., the scientists of today are doing their best to gain insight into the powers of the body and brain in order to have the ability to adjust and utilise this power. There is nothing wrong with this, as long as it is for the greater good of all, and it is, of course, human nature to use our inner power to understand all other aspects of power. We are, after all, the ultimate 'power' so it is therefore quite reasonable for us to imagine that we can conquer all things, indeed I believe it is true that we *can* conquer all things. There are, however, elements within us that to this day we still do not fully comprehend.

Take the current research on stem cell manipulation. Doctors and scientists are beginning to understand that the body is able to recreate itself in ways that may allow for new organs to be grown and used to assist patients with liver failure or kidney replacements, amongst other things. Cells within the body are being used as hosts to house anti-cancer cells in order to help the body fight the disease and restore the body to former good health. We are also discovering that the brain works in wondrous ways, is developing at rates we never understood before and changing according to our experiences and things we are exposed to. The other fascinating thing about the brain is the way that it is able to make connections and store new information that enables us to function in spite of conditions and adversities that might have hindered the process. There is also talk of life experiences that hinder the development of the brain and cause synapses to be formed or not formed which influence the pathways of the brain. These synapses are grooves that are etched into the brain and act as street lanes to other parts of the brain to enhance our ability or close down our capacity, depending on the route that the brain takes as a means of preserving our wellbeing. The brain does this, of course, without conscious direction from us. Its purpose is to preserve life and, I think, to ensure quality of life, but maybe the conscious man/woman's definition of 'quality of life' is different from that of the mind, body and spirit. However, more will be revealed as the doctors and scientists progress their studies into this field and utilise their power of curiosity to discover more about our unconscious inner power.

Perceived power is not false power. It is just power that is dependent on others outside of yourself and therefore prone to change and ineffectiveness.

Inner power is a whole different story. Inner power is always consistent and never changing in its fundamental form of constantly being able to achieve its task despite outward conditions or circumstances. If one is conscious of the power they have within, then they are powerful, even when dressed in tired old pyjamas or while they are in the shower or fast asleep. The power does not shift and is capable of great things that can change one's circumstances and indeed one's sense of mood or mental state. The inner power is the only force that can have a direct effect on the cells in the body or the synapses in the brain, something 'man' is still attempting to comprehend.

So, what is the great inner power that answers to 'no one' or 'no thing'? Well it does answer to someone and that someone is you and only you. Each of us has the key to that power button within us and no other person can access it or make use of it, unless of course we push the button for another person, as the keen followers in the boys' gang might do. You will often hear people say 'don't give your power away'—you cannot in fact give your power away, but you can, however, choose not to use it or allow another to make use of it through you. In other words, if I decide, for whatever reason, to permit someone else to dominate me—and I do this from a position of perceived powerlessness, rather than a choice to be dominated at this time—then I have given my power over to someone else. If, on the other hand, I am sure that by allowing the other to dominate me I will gain great benefits, then I am choosing from my position of personal and inner power to let that happen. This may be the case if faced with a task I have no knowledge of, such as rock climbing, or I might allow another to be dominant as a gift to them in that moment. Such a gesture does not mean that I have lost sight of my inner power; it just means that I choose not to press my inner power button at that time. However, in the very next second, I could choose to press it if I think it wise and I am aware that I have that ability.

Those who have had the misfortune to experience domestic violence and have escaped from that situation will have a clear understanding of what I am talking about. Within an abusive relationship someone often loses the ability to make constructive use of their inner power and finds themselves in a position whereby the abuser's power is dominant. They forfeit their use of their inner power, often as a coping and survival strategy, just as I might do if I were to find myself on the side of a high mountain with very little skills of how to manoeuvre safely without giving over control and power to the skilled climber. If at any point the victim of domestic violence decides that it is no longer a good strategy to give over their power, they have the capacity to press that inner, consistent, always present and effective button of power within them, and it will always respond to their command.

If this inner power is always there and available to us, then why are so many of us feeling powerless and at the mercy of life's circumstances and situations? It is my view that the reason for this is that we fail to appreciate the extent and easy access of this power and therefore spend our lives acting as though we do not have it.

During my career as a social work manager, I had the opportunity to work at a residential and rehabilitation centre for those with brain injury. The users were mainly young men who had had car or motorcycle accidents. Many had been in comas for days or even weeks, some had lost physical ability and/or mental or emotional ability. What was fascinating about this group of young people was their resilience and ability to heal to such a degree that most could and would make every effort to communicate and re-learn simple skills so that they could once again do more for themselves. The other thing that was really interesting was how the brain would filter out information that it did not believe existed. One young man who resided in this unit had some brain damage. He was able to see out of both eyes, but his brain only acknowledged images on his right side, so if you were to show him a circle on a piece of paper and ask him to copy this, he would draw half a circle, as in his world the other half did not exist and he just did not see it. The skilled staff, therapists and doctors at the brain injury centre were confident that with time and hard work on the young man's part they could help him to re-learn to recognise the complete picture of the world.

This ability of the brain to scan out aspects of the world that the rest of us take for granted is not unique, indeed all babies have to learn to acknowledge the entire world and do so through experience and exposure to different things and circumstances. Young babies are not aware that things exist once they are out of sight, so if you were to move something out of their sphere of view the young child would believe it to be gone or no longer in existence. That is why the game peek-a-boo is so much fun—one second, its there, the next second it's gone. The child of approximately six months old would drop something and might well cry for it but would not bother to look for it as they would presume it to no longer be in existence. Whereas the nine-month-old child will look around and down in the direction where it fell, as they now have a sense that things that are out of sight may well exist somewhere, even if they cannot see them. The inner power is just the same, just because you cannot see it does not mean that it does not exist or cannot be located in your world and utilised for your greater good and, who knows, maybe for the good of others.

Your inner power is able to create everything that you can possibly imagine and bring that thing into your life. However, having power is not all of the story. You can press the power button at any time, but it would be really useful to know how to use it once you have put it into action, and that is the part that is really exciting.

So, we have established that we can all access our own inner power. Now we need to discover just how to press that button.

In order to manifest what we want in our lives, be this material things, spiritual awareness or emotional stability, we are required to pay a price. This price is never anything that we cannot afford and is usually something only the individual could pay, such as a unique skill or ability that we can share with others, or reaching out to somebody who would not appreciate this gesture from any other, e.g., the special attention only a father could give to his child or the words of support from a dear friend. We have all been in situations where we are aware that it is the quality of our relationship that makes the difference to the interaction with another. This experience can also be discovered with total strangers who we may meet in passing. You see, the reality is the chances are they are not total strangers after all, but others we have some energetic connection with, and as we meet, this connection is re-experienced.

Life is always about giving and receiving. When we are able to give of ourselves, it is like plugging in the mobile phone in order to recharge it. Each time we give freely and with good intentions, we send a massive energy boost to our ability to receive, and we put ourselves in readiness for the greater good that is ours to enjoy. It is at this point that our inner power is most potent and effective. Remember, this is not about giving to get, it is more like giving your body tasty food for the pleasure and wisdom of eating it and then receiving all the great nutrients and energy from it. Some of us spend a great deal of time giving to others and are often left feeling 'what do people ever do for us?'—it is OK to think this, but it is not wise to dwell on it. If you are giving far too much of yourself, take note that you are choosing to do this. I know there is pressure due to roles and responsibilities that makes you feel that you have to give, even when you do not want to. But it is true that you always have a choice. The possible consequences may lead you to think that you do not have much of a choice, yet all the same, there are always options. Unless someone is dependent on you for their survival you really do have choices. For example, a mother all alone looking after a baby may say in all truth, "At this point, I have no choice but to care for this baby as this child is depending on me to sustain its life and wellbeing." The emphasis in this statement should be on the words 'at this point'. In the very next moment, something could change the circumstances and her choices might be different. If you find yourself in a predicament whereby you feel that the dependency of another is forcing you to give of yourself beyond your greater wishes, then acknowledge that this is a choice for the moment and you will plan to change that situation as and when the appropriate moment arises. This is a significant statement to make as it tells your unconscious mind that this current situation is for a time that will pass, so your mind can then start preparing for the new situation whereby you do not feel compromised or as though you are giving more than you would like.

By honouring our personal feelings, we are giving to ourselves and that is the most important thing we can do, as without you in your world and experience, there really is nothing.

The other extreme of not giving to ourselves is attempting to give far too much to others. This is not only exhausting but is more like overcharging the mobile phone, only to find that the battery is irreversibly damaged and sapped of energy, unable to hold a full charge. This happens to us as well if we attempt to be the superman or woman for others. Often people give too much of themselves out of a sense of guilt or a feeling of unworthiness unless they are doing for others. When one is constantly making themselves available to the use of others, this is not aligned to the universal law of giving and receiving, as one is not allowing space and time to personally receive. To give relentlessly not only robs the giver but also hinders the receiver from giving, as the constant giver is not in a position to receive so the outcome is a blockage in the energy field. A bit like trapped wind in the gut, something needs to shift in order for things to clear and allow a natural flow.

Understanding this process of giving to self as well as to others in accordance with the natural law is a crucial lesson in relation to living one's life and achieving one's full potential in a balanced and comfortable fashion.

I learned this lesson at a time when all I really wanted was to love and be loved. In January of 2003, I was feeling beautifully overwhelmed with great expectations. Spiritually I was in a great place; I had joined the Interfaith Seminary and was on the path to becoming an interfaith minister. I was meeting with like-minded people on a regular basis, we would chant, pray, meditate and debate different spiritual philosophies and this was fantastic, I felt energised and alive. In turn, I had so much joy within that I just wanted to make everyone I encountered happy. I attempted to do this by giving advice and assistance wherever I could. I would offer to help at every opportunity and would not take no for an answer until my offer of help was accepted. I recall visiting my cousin who had a boil on his face, I suggested all types of remedies for this and even offered to administer the natural home remedy I had suggested. He then became quite upset and asked me to leave him alone, he stated that he was fine, but oh no, I insisted on helping him at which point he said in a very sharp and angry tone, "It's my boil and I will do what I want with it, so leave it." At that point I heard him and understood something that I think many may have been trying to convey to me for some time. People just want to be left to live the lives they have chosen, and they really do not appreciate others imposing their desires on to them without invitation or consent. I, of course, was very hurt; after all, I was only trying to help because I cared about him and thought I had something to share. This situation caused me to reflect on the many recent experiences of loved ones telling me to back off and leave them to live their lives. I apologised to my cousin and made light of the situation in order not to burden him or others in the room with my deeply felt pain and rejection at the time. Having respected his wishes, I changed the subject and stayed a reasonable amount of time to not appear rude and then left.

I arrived home still in deep thought as to why so many were not welcoming of my help. Here am I with so much to share and all I want to do is assist them in improving their current situations. Indeed, one friend even said to me, "Why do you always come to my house and wash my plates?" This made me a little angry and my instinct was to reply, "So why do you always have dirty plates for me to wash?" But I resisted that negative thought and simply said in a calm and carefree voice, "Oh I like washing plates." I was offering all my wisdom, ability and knowledge, by saying, here please make use of all I can give and share, this is something I want you to have. But in subtle and not so subtle ways, friends and family were saying they did not need me. The reality was, it was I who needed to be needed and was asking them to fulfil that role for me. That reality hit me so hard. It was like colliding with a ton of bricks and shattered my self-image as this strong, independent go-getter who did not need anything or anybody.

After a painstaking, tearful night of really looking at myself and all that I had become, I realised that all those people, friends and family that I was reaching out to in the guise of 'let me help you', were all mirroring back to me this image of independence and the fantasy that I held of not needing anyone or anything. Finally, at around 2am on that sleepless night, all alone in my bedroom, the penny dropped—I became aware of the fact that yes indeed I need others and want to be useful to others in order to give me a sense of purpose. I decided, in that moment, that my happiness and my peace of mind was purpose enough and I would respect their wishes and no longer impose myself on them, uninvited, again.

Once I made that shift in my thinking and told myself that there was no one to be angry with or upset with, having allowed myself to see the blessing in the situation, I was mentally free to move on with my life. I affirmed that I was ready for a new experience whereby I was content and happy and not so unconsciously needy, and that I could be with people who really needed my help and could give that help from a place of balance and acceptance of my own needs. Most importantly, I decided to choose to believe that it is ok not to give all the time. Once you master the universal lesson of giving and receiving in a balanced way to self and others, amazing things happen. The very next morning, I awoke, in a fairly good mood and a little resigned to the fact that I had agreed to behave differently around others and to practise respecting their wishes and not imposing my self-righteous fix-it attitude onto them. I got up and pottered around the house cleaning and such, telling myself it was OK to just be and that I did not need to plan how I would be of service to others immediately.

At ten that morning the phone rang, and I heard a voice that I had not heard in about a year, saying to me, "Aqualma, will you please consider coming to New Zealand for only six months, as a consultant, we need your expertise." I smiled and said, without hesitation, "Yes, I will come as soon as possible."

Well, my ex-manager who had previously asked me to join her was shocked at my clear and unwavering response. She then said what has changed? Before, you were reluctant to leave your family, as you said they needed you. I replied, "They will be just fine without me and right now your need is greater."

That very afternoon, I had begun to sort out the passport and all the paperwork as I was ready to go where I was meant to be. And, ironically, without the experience of feeling rejected and not needed by family and friends, I would never have had the deep reflective thoughts and may not have been ready to say yes to an opportunity that has enhanced my life beyond all measure.

Your inner power will do all it can to work in line with the thoughts that you give most energy to, so be careful what you concentrate on. It has a way of manifesting in your life.

When you are not following your spirit or making positive use of your inner power, you are likely to feel a little out of sorts and just not comfortable within yourself. If it goes on for too long, one may even feel physically ill or emotional stressed as well as mentally depressed. Such feelings are a sign of being out of alignment with the natural energies that encompass your person and all that is around and about you. It is like swimming against the current, to a degree where you are totally exhausted and weak. This situation may manifest itself in several different ways, from low moods to headaches, etc. If you experience any of this and you have had the situation medically checked out, then you need to ask yourself: what I can do to get back into alignment? One of the best things you could do is anything physical. We spend so much time in a state of body consciousness which means that, whatever happens to us, our bodies are often the first thing to show signs of affect, then our minds, then what is happening in our lives. If we want to change things in our lives, it is often easier to start that change process with the body. Exercise of any type is really a great place to start. It helps the body to feel like it is doing something different and prepares the mind for change. Should you be one of those disciplined people who take regular exercise, I suggest you try a different type of exercise, sport or dance. I'll give you a little hint about something I do to propel that change into action as quickly as possible.

While you are exercising or taking your daily walk, just chant a positive affirmation as you are doing your thing, something like *I am fit, healthy, and all is fine in my world.* Say your chosen words over and over again. This is a really powerful technique, as, while you are exercising, it is hard to harbour negative thoughts because you are mainly concentrating on the physical task. The other very powerful aspect of this chanting while physical activity takes place is that you are at a high energy level due to the exercise, which raises your positive emotions and gives further emphasis and power to the words you are chanting. Once you have chosen your words, try not to think about them in any great depth, concentrate on your breathing, and use the words to maintain rhythm while you complete your exercise task. This practice can shift stuff in your life in such a short space of time, you may not be fully ready to receive, and if that is the case, you will not be in a place to make good use of the opportunity so keep that tip until you feel a little better within yourself and are more prepared to receive.

# Chapter 13

## The Power of Sexual Energy and its link to Creative Spiritually.

In order to plant the seeds for this great lesson, let me just pose a few questions.

- What is sexual energy?
- What does sexual energy have to do with spirituality?
- How might sexual energy impact on our lives?
- Why address this issue of sexual energy?
- What might happen if sexual energy is not used positively, or at all?
- How does one harness sexual energy?
- How is sexual energy used positively?

The question of sexual energy goes to the heart of passion, ambition, desire and clear intention. It is a magnificent force and was designed that way to ensure that human beings procreate and that we are forever replenishing our existence on the earth, as goes for all creatures on this earth. Sexual energy is a powerful feeling that rises from the pit of the stomach and covers the whole body, encouraging immediate action with the promise of fulfilment and relief.

It would be wrong to talk about the force of inner power and enhancing our spiritual energy levels without mentioning the very important topic of sexual energy if we consider that sex, or the lack of it, plays a crucial part of most adults' lives and all teenage fantasy.

Even children have sexual energy, which is why it is so important that they are protected from those who would abuse and exploit them. A child's sexual energy is wrapped up in their sense of curiosity, excitement, purity and total innocence to life's wonders. Hence, they are so accepting of others. This childhood wholeness is a precious thing that should never be tarnished with the impure thoughts, deeds or actions of a fragmented and out-of-control adult with no appropriate boundaries. It is my view that to take advantage of a child in an abusive way, be it sexually or otherwise, is to commit spiritual suicide. But that is a subject for a whole different book.

OK, so let's briefly explore this topic of positive sexual energy. Sexual energy is no different from any other type of energy. It is simply a path of expressing energy and often a chosen path because of the physical and emotional pleasure that it gives. Nothing is created without energy, no thought or action or painting, and I could go on, but energy is always available to us, and in reality, it is how we choose to interpret and make use of this energy that matters. Those of us who are highly successful have learnt how to transform sexual energy into other forms of creation. Let me explain.

My brother, God rest his soul, would often say after experiencing something amazing that it was 'like a sexual experience'. He was describing the rush of exhilarating feelings, the exciting anticipation of what would unfold, the hope of succeeding and being satisfied. This very same feeling can be aroused if one is creating a computer programme, or drawing a picture, or planning a business proposal, or writing a best seller. The sexual energy feelings are borne out of focusing inner creative power and harnessing a method of bringing it to a place where it manifests as something practical, tangible and real. Hence, it comes out of the place of fantasy and into a place of reality and leaves a powerful sense of achievement. Those who are highly motivated, success driven and committed to using their inner energy to create, know the art of transforming sexual energy and often find it hard to verbally express what they feel when going through this process, as this society likes to confine the fullness of sex—and all that it does—to the bedroom or sordid world of perversion. In order to utilise sexual energy effectively one needs to have intense self-control and the ability to remain focused while experiencing powerful feelings of love, pleasure and enthusiasm. However, in spite of the daily efforts of people who are driven by sexual energy, and often successful, to hide the real force that drives them, it is quite apparent. Many of us can identify with the attraction towards the powerful man or woman who has achieved. It is the reason why a self-made man is often sexier and more attractive than a man who is born into money. It is the reason why powerful women are envied and desired by many. The unspoken thing in the air is the intangible existence of sexual power that floats around them. It is the energetic charge of pure creativity that is enhanced by such a person.

What do we need to do to develop and make positive use of our sexual energy? Well, first of all, we need to understand that sexual energy and spirituality are inextricably linked. They are both powerful entities that we have very little understanding of, but when we give them thought and bring them to consciousness, they are able to bring great joy and feelings of fulfilment into our lives.

Both spirituality and sexuality demand that we remain in control of our, emotions, actions and thoughts lest we run the risk of ruining others' lives and rendering ourselves prone to negativity or failing health issues. Both expressions of energy demand self-control and discipline if we are to benefit from the goodness that they can bring to our lives. Mother use to say, when making mention of how couples date and become intimate, "Young people nowadays do not go out, they just come in and what does that leave for tomorrow." She was making reference to the lack of courting that young people indulge in and the quickness with which young people become involved in sexual relations. I have interpreted that what she was saying was this—that if you rush into intimacy, or sex, you fail to leave space for the creative development of that experience. Therefore. you leave very little room for growth of the situation. And things that are meaningful, powerful and successful require space and time, for us to grow and get to know it, so that it can become all that it is. In other words, spiritual and sexual energy require time, space and positive expression to manifest into their fullness. This is true of babies in the womb, a successful business, a meaningful relationship and a greater understanding of self.

As consenting adults, what we do, think and imagine sexually plays a big part in the thought process and hence the power of the mind to create or destroy our life's experiences. We talked earlier of the importance of positive energies and the impact of emotion in relation to the thought process. Well, in the midst of passion, we have all the ingredients to create powerful thoughts, yet this is often a time when we decide that thinking is not the main aim and we waste those opportunities to create constructively.

However, sexual energy can also be utilised *outside* of the intimate experience with another and this takes time and careful learning to understand the process. Let me say that again—sexual energy does not have to be used only for a sexual act. Have you noticed when a great idea comes to mind and you instantly start thinking how to put that idea into action, there is a warm, exciting, almost overwhelming feeling in the pit of your stomach that quickly turns into something requiring action? Some may even feel a sensation of pleasure in the genital area. Most of us do not react to this feeling as it seems slightly out of sync for an idea rather than for an attraction to another. But if we were to acknowledge this feeling of sexual, energetic charge and use it to enhance the creative visualisation about the idea we have just conjured up, we would give the idea such a powerful force, it would truly manifest in no time at all.

As you can see, the subject of sexual energy is vast and could take up most of this book. So now that some salient questions have been posed at the start of the chapter, and one idea about how to use it has been shared, I will leave it to your creative minds to consider when and if you are ready to embrace the answers. All will be revealed, so that you can make best use of your personal sexual energy.

Before we close this subject, I would like to share with you something I learnt whilst studying with the Interfaith Seminary to become an ordained minister. This lesson was given to us by a minister of many years' standing and in-depth learning of quite a few established religions. He holds an eminent position within his order and is highly respected. However, as he said to us, "Take all learning and decide for yourself what you choose to believe and practice."

He shared with us an old school of thought, which goes something like this: If two consenting adults choose to spend time together in a united sexual relationship, they are not only sharing their bodies and affections, they also take on each other's Karma and or life lessons.

This is deep. On hearing this, it made me think long and hard about who I might choose to share my sexual experiences with and how much I might be willing to take on their life's task as well as mine, not to mention what *my* life task might demand of *them*. My very prestigious Uncle Phineas in Jamaica, the local Justice of the Peace, for the district, would put it far more simply than that. He would say, "If you lie with dogs, you rise with fleas." And he was not just talking about physical cleanliness but more to do with character and position in life. It is one school of thought, and like everything else that we have discussed thus far, take from it what you will and feel free to leave the rest.

The subject of inner power covers many aspects and has many avenues of expression that could either assist in positive use of it or diminish its effectiveness. We have just touched on a few, but this is enough for our purposes of understanding how it assists in the process of positive thought and creative manifestation.

# Chapter 14

## Choices and the Power to Change:

We are one of the most creative animals on the planet, utilising our minds voices and bodies to depict the world around us in ways that constantly amaze. We are the embodiment of the omnipresent force that established the universe and all its powers and order.

Having such innate skill and power is often far beyond the comprehension of many of us so most of us do not utilise our abilities to our full potential, but I believe it is not for all of us to use our full potential, just some of us. The rest of us are required to provide a service that enables others to thrive. It is my opinion that these positions are not foretold or forced upon us. We have a choice. We can take an active part in creating our world or we can decide to just live within the world that others create for us. What have you chosen? Whatever your decision is, you still have the power to change that, and please note, none of the decisions are wrong, as both parties are needed in this time in order to maintain the equilibrium. Balance is crucial in the pattern of the universe and we are an intricate part of maintaining that balance.

The amazing thing about being alive and growing is that we can constantly keep learning and, indeed, our total make-up is about doing just that. Every cell in our body is geared up to renewing itself, our blood has the ability to utilise oxygen to clean itself so that it can improve and perform at peak level. It is within our nature and innate ability to change and grow.

Change and growth can, however, be very scary and most of us resist it, often to our detriment. The universe knows very well when we have grown out of a situation or habit and if we hold on, beyond the time to let go, we risk missing out on an opportunity that could change and shape our lives in wonderful ways. Some say, 'better the devil you know', I say the road of expectation and wonder is far more exciting and ultimately more fulfilling. However, this road can be rocky and painful, to say the least. So, why is change so challenging?

When you embark on a life of spiritual growth the universe will push you, trusting that you will succeed, and will create great situations in your life to test your commitment to growth and change. After a horrendous car accident, that I experienced in Jamaica, when a taxi driver decided to speed, causing serious injury to the other four passengers myself and himself, this left me with a fractured skull, terrible facial injuries and unable to walk for a number of days. I spent three months in Jamaica recovering. On my return to England feeling vulnerable, with no confidence, low and somewhat depressed, the universe found me a job that paid well, that I had the skills to do, but it was up the motorway, in an area with small winding roads that I was terrified to drive down. I was also provided with a car so that I had no excuse not to take up the opportunity to overcome what was an unrealistic fear that I chose to harbour as a result of the near-death car accident some four months earlier.

There I was, faced with a chance to grow and heal or remain stuck in a place of fear and inadequacy. I had previously loved driving and would get in my car and go down any motorway without a second thought, but now I was terrified and challenged to overcome this fear. By the grace of the Most High, I did it and indeed some two years on I am still being tested to venture further and further out in weather conditions that just make me wince. High winds, stormy rain and foggy conditions have challenged me on several journeys. I simply keep repeating 'I am safe and protected always'. Every time I conquer a new battle on the road, my lost confidence slowly but surely re-emerges with a greater, calmer sense of resilience. This level of growth and healing cannot be bought or bottled and is really difficult to describe. It is not euphoria or extreme excitement, but more like a mature acceptance of the fact that I can be so much greater than I am and that this can be safe and comfortable. What a great and reassuring feeling.

So, when life throws you a test of overcoming adversities and a chance to develop greater resilience, know that the universe has confidence in you and will not give you any obstacle that you do not have a 100% chance of overcoming. The only enemy you may possibly have is your own personal self-doubt, which some refer to as the 'devil on your back'. You have control! Pace yourself and take it in your stride, do nothing until you feel ready to do so, and trust that everything you experience is a positive learning curve. This can be hard, I know, when it hurts like hell or brings up a level of fear in you that feels like it will swallow and engulf you in one big breath. It is at such times when we feel totally overwhelmed and unable to see how we might survive or achieve our task, that we must remember that we are greater than the body we reside in and we have the support of the universe which is connected to our higher selves.

# Chapter 15

## Building Resilience: The stuff that makes us bounce back.

It is important that we recognise what helps us to bounce back after falls or failures. We need to understand what gives us the strength to go on and survive when giving up could be an easier option. Well, there are a combination of things that assist in the task of bouncing back, and once we understand what some of these things are, then we have tools to help us in the darkest moments of despair and the vast feelings of overwhelming nothingness. Some of you will know the horrible, isolated and unimaginable inner turmoil that I am referring to. For those of you who do not know this place, I pray you never experience it. Here are some of the things we can do to guard ourselves from it and heal ourselves if we have experienced it in the past or even currently.

**Belonging:** It is in our innate make-up to feel as though we are intrinsically connected to others, we are creatures of a pack and we need to feel that we have alliances with others. These days, when computers and technology are so popular and families are ripped apart through insurmountable stress, poverty, housing laws and war-torn countries and the new societal view that separateness and individuality are the new in-thing, the idea of family and unity in a small nucleus of relatives is so hard to maintain. All the options of being alone are so readily available, such as studio flats, on-line shopping, internet relationships and erosion of traditions that held people connected and involved with each other. Yet despite these aforementioned changes in society, people still find ways to connect with others if they can, through supporting a football team and meeting up at matches, through frequenting a pub and becoming a regular, through joining a weight-watching class, or becoming a gang member.

We crave belonging and need to be a part of what other humans are experiencing. Some achieve this through work associations or church associations, others achieve this by partying on a regular basis. Either way, to do this, we require resources, such as appropriate clothes, disposable income and means of transport. All this costs money that many of us do not have, hence, some struggle to maintain connections with others in this day and age. It is important that we find cheap and economical ways of uniting, as we did in the old days. I recall my parents and older relatives would ritually visit each other at weekends—one weekend it would be our house they all came to, the other weekend we would visit a nearby aunt, and occasionally many of us would go all the way to Birmingham to visit aunts and uncles there. By rotating the visits, the cost was contained as each would provide for the other. In such gatherings, all felt that they had a place to be and belonged to a group of people who recognised and cared for them. Indeed, this tradition was so strong in my family that new-found friends were keen to join the family union, and many did—to this day, they are still welcomed when we now occasionally gather.

It is my view that belonging to a set group of people ignites the earliest feelings of attachment and survival instincts. Being a part of an established group allows us to let our guard down and relax at a level I feel we often fail to appreciate. I have a friend who welcomes a handful of people into his home every Sunday evening and has been doing so for some ten years or more now. When you enter his home, you feel like you belong. It is a space to sit and do nothing, or chat and laugh. You can go there when you are happy, sad or indifferent. When I leave his home, I feel like my batteries have been recharged and that I can face the world for another week with extra protective stuffing. I once attended a spiritual development circle every Friday for three years. This also gave me a sense of belonging and a feeling of being a part of something that mattered. When I lived in New Zealand for a year, I was fortunate to find another spiritual empowerment circle and attended every Monday for the whole year. Again, it felt like family, even though the make-up of the group, consisted of White British settlers (in Zealand), White New Zealanders, Maori men and women, Chinese and Asian group members, and me of course, a woman of African origin, descending from Jamaica and born and raised in Britain. We had all found common, acceptable ground, and in that space, we nourished each other's deepest needs by just allowing each other to be. Being with others also allows us an opportunity to express, via words or actions or simply being there and through expression and sharing we have the opportunity to reflect on who we are and how we are in this world. Armed with such knowledge, we are better equipped to deal with the wider world while maintaining a sense of self and others.

**Feeling valued:** This gives us a sense of purpose and self-worth. When another human being is able to make positive use of our time, energy and abilities, this allows us to know that we are part of something greater than ourselves and enables us to feel connected to others, the world and to life itself. When we share time and space with others, we become aware of our strengths and weaknesses in relation to the characters around us, which helps us to think about who we are and what we would like to be.

Some of us find value and purpose in our service to animals, birds or plant life. All living things have their own energy and power, and when we are connected to any life form, this allows us to connect with universal forces that enhance our very being and help us to grow as individuals.

**Achieving:** To gain something we did not have before, succeed at something that we have never done before, or conquer where we may have failed previously gives us a great feeling that we have the ability to shape our own life and make changes to our reality. It really does not matter if the changes are great or small as long as they allow the individual to feel that something new and/or different has happened in their lives. It is the ability to reach out and stretch ourselves beyond our own skills, knowledge and abilities that allows for a sense of achievement and the wonderful thing about obtaining experiences of success is that it leaves us with a sense that even more can be achieved and that we as individuals can acquire things, thoughts, abilities and knowledge that we never had before. We can gain a sense of future accomplishments because if we can achieve one thing then it is evidence that we have the ability to possibly achieve something else.

Achievements are a great boost for one's sense of self-esteem as they remind us that something else can happen in our lives. So, no matter what we have been through or how hard life gets, if we can achieve something, we have strived for then we become aware that things can change and the negative cloud can be lifted by our very own actions and efforts. We find that we have the power to make a difference in our own lives, for our greater good. We therefore need to remember our achievements when the hard times come, so that we have hope for the future.

When I worked with teenagers in a secure unit, as a manager, when a young person achieved something, such as passing a test in school or gaining rewards for good behaviour that week. I would always tell girls and the boys, how well they had done for achieving what they did and remind them that this was something new that they could put into their benefits bank. I would explain that the benefits bank was a place in their memory where they could keep all the good things that had happened in their lives including their successes and achievements, so that they could call on such memories when they were feeling low. The benefits bank is an idea that I read about in a book by Paulo Coelho, the author of the book The Alchemist. I found the idea of the storing up good life experiences for a rainy day to be so powerful that I now share it in my training sessions with health, education and social welfare professionals, especially when I am presenting on children's mental health issues.

Having good self-belief assists the positive power of thoughts and creates a wonderful sense of inner strength, hence, reflecting on our achievements aids our future positive development, no matter how bleak the past might have been.

**Efficacy:** While delivering a training course on mental health and resilience in children, I asked a group of participants if they understood the meaning of the word efficacy and a man stood up and said, "It's when two cogs come together in motion and enable something else to move, like the machinery inside a clock." This is absolutely right—and in relation to emotional efficacy, we need to do something that allows others to benefit. When a child helps his or her mother to set the dinner table for all the family to have a meal, the child places the plates, knives and forks on the table and then watches the family members sit around the table, pick up the knives and forks and make use of them to eat the meal. The child responds to watching others make use of their table preparations by feeling a sense of usefulness and belonging to a process and experience bigger than themselves. This kindles a feeling of connectedness to others and purpose in life. In fact, the experience of watching and knowing that they have done something that benefits others allows children to know more about the art of giving and receiving in a tangible way. Efficacy can also work for adults. Every time we do something that benefits others, we receive a dose of feel-good hormones (dopamine) that enhance our wellbeing. When we wash up the plates or help with the cleaning up at a friend's or relative's home after a party, after we sit down and observe that all is in order again, we feel comfortable inside, knowing that we have contributed to the wellbeing and satisfaction of others. This is what happens when we do charitable work of any kind and this helps us to know that we matter and are important in the scheme of things. Building efficacy is a powerful way of developing self-confidence and ultimately resilience.

**Effective communication:** To communicate effectively we need to express ourselves in a way that allows others to hear and respond to us positively. This requires us to have a clear sense of what we are trying to say and some understanding of how it will be received by the other party. This also requires some empathy and insight on the part of the person who wishes to communicate effectively. We also need to be prepared to be challenged or questioned before we get the desired result. Most importantly, we must be prepared to listen even if we are not hearing what we want to hear. When speaking to others, we need to be aware that at times it is quite difficult for us to really hear things that might be distressing or cause us some discomfort. The brain has the capacity to shut down and simply block out things that are not easily accepted by the individual, or the memory will very quickly put that experience away so that it is not there in the conscious part of the mind, but will remain as an unconscious memory.

I recall one occasion when I was having a party and my sisters-in-law (common law wives were kicking up quite a fuss about helping my cousin with cleaning and preparing the fish. This was all going to happen on the Saturday afternoon on the same day as the party. That morning I got a phone call from one of the sisters-in-law announcing in quite an anxious and upset voice that my cousin had died. I responded by saying "What? Who is going to cook the fish then?" You see, what my brain did with the information of my cousin's death was to put it away to the back of my brain and focus on what was manageable for me at that time. That is how clever the brain is. My sister-in-law repeated the bad news and I heard it the second time to my absolute distress at losing a wonderful relative.

**Self Tolerance:** this speaks to the parts of us that are accepting or rejecting of ourselves and others**,** for example if we arrive late to a meeting that we really wanted to be on time for, we can often spend time beating ourselves up and deciding in that moment that everything about us is bad, and we are failures unable to achieve anything. We may become very angry with ourselves and quite unforgiving. Where as, if we had self-tolerance, we would look at ourselves differently, probably be less judgemental, while accepting the disappointment that we would be feeling for being late and acknowledging that this too will pass. We would let ourselves off the hook and strive forward with our day, remembering that this particular experience of being late, does not define us.

The art of loving ourselves includes accepting that we will disappoint ourselves and have habits and ways that we don't like and that there are something's about ourselves that we would like to change. It is important that we reflect on who we are and what we like or dislike about our character, behaviour and physical being. Then we can start doing work on accepting the parts of us that we cannot change, such as our height or our history.

In order to have inner tolerance we also have to be able to strip back every incident to its fundamental importance, so that when we are feeling frustrated, angry or disappointed in ourselves or others, we can react with a view that is proportionate to the situation, so if a friend has spilt a class of red wine on your lovely cream carpet, we may feel very little tolerance towards them and that action, however if we can remember that the red wine is only a colouring on the carpet and in this day and time we have things that can correct such an error, we then realise that we have no real loss. it the moment however we may get to thinking why did he or she do that, was it to upset or hurt me, or are they just so clumsy and is this the type of person I wish to be socialising with, all because of a little red wine. At this point we would need to take a deep breath and practice some empathy maybe by asking ourselves, how might that person be feeling now and what can I do to help them feel better, that would be an expression of tolerance and we have to feel that tolerance inside of us, before we can express it on the outside.

Inner tolerance is not about enduring or putting up with disrespect from others. In the event that you have been empathetic to someone and considered their views, you still find that person to be disregarding or rude towards you, then I suggest you name what you are feeling from a place of consideration and calmness and then tell them how it feels to you, depending on their response you can decide how you behave or relate to that person in future. It may be wise to avoid such people if you can, or limit the amount of time you spend with them, but always remember that when a person is being rude or disrespectful towards you, this is an expression of their pain and the stuff they are trying to make sense of, within themselves in a very confused and horrible way, but it is not personal to you, and may just be away of them having a break from the turmoil and distress that they are feeling on the inside of them, it is a distraction of their pain, just like over drinking, over eating and abusing drugs. I am not saying you should pity them, just do not allow their stuff to cloud your staff and we need to appreciate that they are probably doing the best they can, as Louise Hay would say, in her book love yourself heal your life.

**Hopefulness:** psychologist have written about the idea of those who are more hopeful, being healthier happier and possibly living longer, but how does one become more hopeful. I think the first thing we should do is try to understand what our fears, doubts and worries might do for us. Fear doubt and worry are there as warning signs to be acknowledged and acted upon to keep safe and secure, they are not there to be dwelled upon. If I am about to give a public talk and I become conscious that I am feeling some anxiety of apprehension, I then allow myself to feel that feeling, I try to locate where I am feeling it, could it be in my head or stomach and I don't ask why I am feeling it, because that would be dwelling upon it. The next thing I do is think about what action I can take to diminish this feeling. What works for me is reading over my notes, looking at myself in a mirror and telling myself that I am ok and I know what I am doing, I remind myself that I have done it before if indeed I have, if not I think of all the transferable skills that I can bring to this situation. Then I remember that

I am not alone and I have universe of positive energy that will be working with me and I trust to that.

Hope is expecting the best and believing that you are worthy of it in spite of what may have happened in the past. Sometimes when dreadful things happen to us, we cope by telling ourselves that next time we will be ready and this leaves us in a state of expecting worse and not preparing for something better. I have learned to flip the script and tell myself 'that is done' and I am ready for better things now'. I know that I have the power to create a better future for myself and so I spend my time taking steps towards it, rather than dwelling on what has hindered or hurt me in the past. Of course this is never easy, but to practice on a regular basis and being prepared to forgive yourself when you have failed to remain positive is a good recipe for success and the ability to hold on to hopefulness.

We can also hold on to hope for others, this is something good parents do all the time. The parent will remain optimistic about what the child might achieve, then the parent will champion the cause for that child, which in turn gives that child an alternative view of themselves, that they just might believe one day. When I work with vulnerable young people, I try to find something positive in their live experience or character and reflect this back to them, stating that there are good things about them and they can use these things to progress in the future, I believe this about them and if they can hold on to that then maybe they can have hope for their futures and know that they are not alone.

# Chapter 16

## To Trust is to Take a Chance

In life, it is important that we offer ourselves the opportunity to experience more and more wonderful things and, in order to do so, we have to take some chances. Now I am not suggesting that you be reckless, but it is important to weigh up the odds and take calculated risks in order to discover—or with the hope of discovering—something new and hopefully exciting or enlightening.

When I first started public speaking, I did not know what it was to speak publicly to over two hundred people, but I took a chance. I ensured that I had an excellent understanding of the subject I would be talking on, I also prepared well, by learning something of my audience, then getting to the venue early to set up and most importantly eating and sleeping well so that I was physically and mentally ready, then I took a chance and did something I had never done before. During my first public talk I felt, nervous and excited but I remain focussed on the task and trusted that all was in order. I know deliver public talks with a limited level of nervousness and a knowledge that I know what I am doing and can do it well. I also appreciate that things may go wrong such as the microphone may not work, or the PowerPoint may fail, yet I know that I have all that I need within me to deliver a good talk and all other things are just extra security.

By taking a chance of becoming a public speaker, I have been able to assist thousands of professionals and others to safeguard children and improve their own professions and life's.

The most important chance one can take is to try and change oneself, to make efforts to adopt new habits and change old behaviours into desired practices, to live differently and embrace new ways of being. |In order to make real differences in our life's we need to decide to take a chance on being the person we really think we are, and not playing to the script that others might have given us, or living within the limitations of our class, culture or community experiences. We have to decide to step out of our comfort zones and venture forward into realms that may appear alien to us. This is the purpose of many people's life's, for others it may be enduring what we know. the question is are you ready to take a chance to find out what is out there for you and accept the outcome of what might happen. Remember you are never alone and the universe will support you in all your efforts to grow and progress, for that is the path of the universe to change and develop into its greatest self.

# Chapter 17

# The Spiritual Teachings in New Zealand.

As night draws near and silence unfolds in the dark space around us, a certain peace envelops the mind if only we can allow ourselves to surrender to it. I knew that I needed a change in life, but I was unsure of what that change would be. Suddenly, while sitting in my wonderful seven bedroom house, my spirit told me that change must come. I attempted to meditate in order to find an answer to my searching question of what next. I hoped for some guidance or maybe a small blessing or miracle. In the past, amazing things had happened for me after meditating for just a short while so I was filled with great anticipation of what spirit might produce. I was feeling low, unloved and somewhat unwanted by those around me. I just wanted to be useful to myself and others. Feeling confused and disappointed with those around me, I now decided to depend on spirit and the grace of the Most High to enable me to find purpose in life.

What is a spiritual experience? Some would describe it as something that is out of the ordinary, packed with weird and wonderful events that leave you feeling uplifted and with a renewed trust in life. For some this would be true, but this does not stop other experiences being spiritual.

One day when I was feeling lost and alone in England, my friends and relatives appeared to be tired of my over-helpful, interfering ways. I remember saying to myself, "I wish I was somewhere else, anywhere else would do, where people might appreciate me." The very next morning, the phone rang. It was an ex-colleague, Angie. She had called all the way from New Zealand and enquired if I would like to come over as a consultant and work in a new secure unit that had recently opened. Without a second thought, I said yes. The next few months consisted of planning and preparing. Many obstacles appeared, such as the difficulty I experienced with renting my home in Kent. But I refused to let anything stand in my way. I was going to New Zealand one way or the other.

The day had finally arrived, and I was on the plane to this far-off land, filled with anticipation and excitement. What would I find in this distant land? Would I have an amazing spiritual experience? Would the Maori people really be as spiritual as I was led to believe?

Well, I had been in New Zealand for two months and yes, the Maori people were even more spiritual than I was led to believe, but as well as this, many of the other people are also very spiritual. I found a lovely little Christian spiritualist church and had the opportunity to do a service and evidence some clairvoyance. I had joined an open circle ran by an English woman who moved to New Zealand with her husband in the late 1960s and who has been running a circle for about 30 years. Oh, and at work I had been delivering training workshops on positive thinking to young people and acting as a coach and consultant to staff. I felt truly appreciated and most welcomed in Auckland NZ. There was a part of me that did not want to go home and another part that desired to go home as I thought my family were missing me at least a little. Another part of my spiritual journey, as I mentioned earlier, is to accept that people really can do just fine without me.

In New Zealand I found that I had time to spend my evenings meditating or reading up on spiritual matters. This for me had been a great opportunity to just reaffirm my sense of spirituality and to be clearer about my path

I had also discovered that I felt really connected to the Most High and I wanted to continue growing, spiritually. The dreams I got were quite powerful and I am still working them out, but I know they will be revealed to me, all in good time.

So there I was in New Zealand fulfilling many of my lifelong dreams. I had begun exercising on a regular basis and am even contemplating piano lessons. I tell you, when one achieves most of their live goals this is really scary because it leads one to think, well what is next and if there is nothing, does that mean it is time to die? I am sure there is more. Indeed, by that

Time I had not met my soul mate as yet and done the unity thing with a man of my dreams, so there most definitely was something more to live for.

This experience of being in New Zealand has taught me so much and exposed me to such happiness that it is almost mind blowing. Thank you, my blessed Mother, Father, Most High God.

There is so much truth in the saying 'you never know what you've got, until it's gone'. Yes, it is true. I had the time of my life and indeed I have learnt to appreciate my roots in such a fundamental way. I have come to see my experience of being Jamaican as so dear to my heart. I long to hear the language again and sit in the way I am accustomed to with people like myself, talking and socialising. I recall I phoned my son back in England and was telling him of my plans to stay on in New Zealand and maybe move to another part of the country. He said, just as my mother would have, "Tek time waalk—hard." I knew exactly what he meant and could almost hear my mother saying it. The saying means do go for what you want but be very careful in the process, or in other words 'go forward with vigour, but be aware of possible dangers'. When someone says this to you, they are saying in the most loving and caring way they can that you should be cautious, but do not let that stop you. My Maori new found sister and friend might have said, "Sister, and I say this to you with much love—go for it, but be wise, eh?"

Jamaicans are very good at saying a great deal in the fewest of words with such deep and elaborate meaning. The tone of voice that is used also says a great deal. In my son's few words, I could hear him expressing his concern and slight worry about my adventures and yet the hope in his voice that I would do the right thing. God Bless that child. He is like a mother, father and angel all wrapped up in one. I love him with everything I have got and constantly thank the Lord for him. When I heard my English born son of a Grenadian father born to a Jamaican mother speak in such a natural Jamaican tongue, I could feel the presence of the ancestors in that moment. I burst out laughing on the phone and said to him, "Oh, it is so good to hear that raw Jamaican Lord your grandmother instantly came to life again through you." He laughed too and then we continued to have a swift and joking rapport in Jamaican: 'Wat a ting, eeh sah, de Jamaican talk sound so sweet. I miss yu, so yu cee." It is only by stepping away from what is so close that we realise just how much we appreciate it. I imagine it is the same in terms of loving God—it is in the moments when we feel alone and empty that we actually remember the loving that God gives us.

Well, I was still in New Zealand some five months after I arrived. One morning at 6am I was awakened by a cousin ringing me for the first time. I did not think oh my God what is wrong? I thought she was ringing because I had left a message wishing her a happy birthday. She made polite conversation and then said, "Oh, I have bad news, about T." I could not hear her properly and said, "Who P, and God forbid anything should happen to my son." She repeated, "Cousin T in Jamaica." At that moment I felt instant relief and then sudden shock. "What happened?" I asked. She explained that he was ill and in hospital but seemed to have recovered well. My cousin who had called kept checking out how I was, and I assured her that I was fine. I had started to break the apartment rule by smoking a cigarette in the premises but other than that I was fine. I put the phone down and instantly started to pray for my dear cousin T. Then I remembered the dream I had had two nights before. I dreamt that I was at a hospital with some Rasta's that I did not know, we were visiting someone. I could not see who the sick person was nor was I sure that we were visiting one particular person. There were some stuffed toys about and one stuffed monkey. A white person (man) came and made a joke, all the Rasta's laughed out of politeness, but we all really thought he was being a little rude. Then we left the hospital and went to a big gathering that seemed like a party outdoors with several rooms indoors with things happening.

In the dream my family were now present, and we were about to leave in a small car. Then my locks started falling out in long chunks, I commented that my hair had never fallen out like this before. We were to drive through what seemed like a small gate. I said the car would never fit through it and I was told it was OK because they had fixed the gate. As we drove forward the two sides of the gate opened so we could fit through. Then a young woman who looked like she was dressed to party, with hardly any clothes on, said to me, "Could you keep this for me?" I said, "What is it?" and she showed me her knickers. She had tried to put them in a cupboard, but all the cupboards had food in them. She wrapped the knickers in a plastic bag and said, "If I put this in the fridge, will it be

OK?" I told her to give them to me and I would find somewhere to keep them for her. At that point I woke up.

The interesting thing about this dream is that T was a Rasta and used to have very long locks down his back. When he became ill, he cut them off but, in his heart, he was still a Rasta. He told me when I was 15 years old that it is not the hair that makes someone a Rasta, but the locks in their heart. My dream was warning me about Cousin T's passing, and I think the knickers part represented some scandal, as plastic carrier bags in Jamaica are referred to as scandal bags as you can see right through them. I think the fact that the cupboards were full of food represents that we still have abundance in spite of the possible shame and scandal that might arise. The gateway being open represents going into a new dimension, one we never thought we would be able to achieve. I think the death of T will herald a time of amazing change and revelation for many. There may be a period of struggle beforehand, but things will work out for the best in the end.

Oh, the power of dreams! This is so amazing that I just keep praying for clarity in understanding and interpreting the dreams. I spoke to a friend about the dream who said, "Oh yes, hair falling out always represents death, a lady told me that many years ago." I spend a great deal of time trying to work out the meaning of dreams after I have written them out first thing on waking. Usually the dream reveals itself to me and then, in a flash, the dream makes sense. I think these types of dreams are just to prepare you rather than act as a revelation to you.

I have done so much in terms of spiritual growth since being in New Zealand that it is amazing. On one occasion in New Zealand, I went to a university to meet with a new-found friend who lectures there. She had invited me to lunch in their very nice and spacious canteen. As I ordered my food, she informed me that she would not be eating as she was fasting. She spoke while I ate. Noni talked of her fast as a method of connecting in a purposeful way with God. She informed me that her mother had taught her to be still in the silence. Noni went on to explain how she usually goes to God with a banquet-sized table of requests, but recently she has learned to be more specific and focused as to what she would ask for. On that occasion, she started her prayer with gratitude and humbleness. She then made her request and asked God to answer her.

As she waited for God's response, she described this as the silence. The silence can mean no signs or symbols or no voice from God. This is the long wait for a sign that one's prayer has been heard and will be answered. On occasions, the answer from God can come in many different ways, i.e., via something someone says, a page in the Bible or other books, the words or actions of children around you, or even something you might see on TV, or face book message that stands out for you. In her explanation of observing the silence, I recalled the vision I had of the beautiful small African Lady, who told me that I should learn to listen to the silence. The lessons I have been experiencing and learning from, suddenly became clear to me. The impatience that I had was waiting for God to answer my wishes. God had been enabling me to understand that if I can wait on this holy force then I can wait for anything, and that is the revelation: the silence is the waiting period. Listening to the silence means finding sense in that process that is setting the path for the blessings. I feel truly enlightened and maybe I have not explained it very well. Hopefully, as I understand it more, I will be able to explain it better, praise Jah, the Most High, Yahweh, the Universal force.

# Chapter 18

## The Material and Spiritual Journey to my Physical Home

The thought of getting on a plane was too totally terrifying, but it had to be done, sooner or later. How long was I going to live in fear of yet another disaster in a country or island very far from home. The car accident I had in Jamaica was constantly playing on my mind and the whole idea of getting on a plane again just reminded me of the severe panic attack I had on the plane when returning from Jamaica, but here I am deciding to live, and that means getting stuck into life again.

While offering a training course for Young Minds on the issue of mental health and young people, one bright young woman, white and slim and keen to progress, looked at me during the break and said, "Your life seems really interesting." I had never thought of my life as interesting, but I decided to play with this idea and give 'living interestingly' a chance. That was it. I decided to take my fears, throw them over my shoulder and never look back.

I went to the travel agent and said, "Give me a ticket to Ghana." This was done and I was already shopping in preparation for the trip. The plan was hatched, and I was psychologically *nearly almost slightly* ready to take this massive courageous leap into what had become my haunting, debilitating, ongoing, not-so-well-hidden fear. This was going to be my way to cleanse myself of the memory of imminent annihilation and certain catastrophic doom. Then spirit sent me the most ultimate and positive enlightened spirit in the form of an amazing person I met briefly at a bus stop some four years ago.

I had been to Birmingham to visit Aunt May and Uncle Dave. It was always a pleasure visiting Aunt May, as she knew how to make you feel like you were always coming home. There would be a cooked light meal, whatever hour you arrived. Back in the old days when she was much younger and fitter, there would also be freshly baked plain and/or fruit cake, believe me, no one made a cake like Aunt May. The texture would be fluffy, with a light brown outer colour and a deep yellow centre. When you sank your teeth into it, the cake would almost melt in your mouth and had this amazing flavour that just made you want more and more. Just like the creamed potatoes she used to give us when we were children. My brothers and I loved the biannual trip that seemed like such a long way away in my dad's small blue car to visit Aunt May and eat those wonderful meals. Mum would pack crisps and sandwiches for the journey, along with tissues and old newspapers, as I was always car sick. (It is said that if you stuff newspaper down the chest, beneath the clothes, this stops car sickness) Of course, we would gobble up all the food, drinks and sweets before we were even half way down the motorway. Mum would remind us to try and count the cows and sheep as we passed them. After a few years, and as we got bigger, we grew tired of this game, but we would still play it, if only in our minds, because cows and sheep were a rare sight in London except for on television. Birmingham was always darker and greyer than London, with big old factory-looking buildings and quaint little houses down very narrow, winding and hilly roads. It seemed like a different world, a bit like the streets in the television show, Coronation Street. I know it is not all like that but that's my memory of it. However, none of that mattered, as once we were on the inside of Aunt May's house, the world was a fairy-tale where there was no wicked witch or monsters, just people who were always pleased to see us and ever so willing to feed us and teach us all sorts of things as well as nurture us. As I got nearer to my teenage years, my parents would put me on the coach to Birmingham to spend my holidays with Aunt May. I believe the thinking behind this was that I would be safe, as my parents both worked and could not supervise their precious little girl over the holidays, and the secondary reason was that I might learn appropriate womanly behaviour and etiquette, such as good housekeeping and cooking skills. Well they succeeded on one count—I was always very safe, but do not ask me to make a cake, or knit a jumper. This I cannot do in spite of Aunt May's gallant efforts to school me in these skills. My dear aunt passed away at the age of ninety three on my son's birthday and although she can no longer makes the cakes, or knit woollen suits, little else has changed, in her house in Birmingham and as the only girl who was sent to Auntie for safekeeping, I got into the habit of being with Aunt May. I have learnt so much from her in terms of life, philosophy, spirituality and value of self. To this day, I still visit the home of Aunt May and Uncle Dave regularly.

Anyway, it was while returning from one of my regular trips to Birmingham that I met this amazing spiritual man who proved to be an absolute Godsend to my life and my material and spiritual journey to myself. There I was at a bus stop in Golders Green, with my little blue pulley suitcase and feeling very tired and sick of travelling after the boring two-hour coach trip back to the London coach depot. In order to break the monotony of the long ongoing wait for the 260 bus to Willesden, I made polite conversation with a calm and well-dressed black man, who stood nearby. He was dressed casually but smart, with a well-worn, soft brown brief case. He wore clothes of quality and stood with dignity. He had locks tied back in a short ponytail, and his dark cocoa complexion looked fresh and healthy, as though he had just returned from a warm, humid climate. I spoke to him about the long boring wait and how much of our lives all this waiting about takes up. He agreed it was no fun waiting but commented that it gives one an opportunity to talk to friendly people. I thought his answer was interesting, so I continued to talk to him. It turned out we were getting on the same bus. Somewhere in the conversation, this intriguing stranger said that he had lived in Ghana for several years and loved it to bits. At this point I got quite excited and as I did not know how far he was going on the bus and how long we had to continue talking, I took out pen and paper and said, "Give me your number. Whenever I get to go to Ghana, I should like to know there is someone there who could introduce me to the country." He replied, "You are most welcome to come stay with my family and me." I explained I did not know which year I would come, hopefully the following one, but I said that any day I intended to get on the plane I would let him know.

I had dreamt of going to Ghana for years and thought I would discover so much more about my ancestry, cultural history and my deep and meaningful African name. I was going to discover more of my soul purpose and link with the natural energy that runs through my veins and guides my thoughts and actions. I saw Ghana as my path to revealing more of me and a doorway to greater spiritual growth. I was not wrong, but what I experienced on this journey to discovery was way beyond anything I could have possibly imagined, dreamt about or desired. Yet the journey all started with what could be described as a chance encounter with a slim black professional man at a bus stop on a dull, dreary, typical English day. Within the past four years, since meeting the wonderful man from Ghana, so many life-changing experiences have taken place for me. Some of these life-changing things have left me with great memories and amazing spiritual prowess, consisting of fun, joy and overwhelming contentment, while others nearly ripped the very soul out of me and threatened to take my sanity, emotional stability and personality with it. Who would think surviving a car accident could really be so devastating? I imagine, only those who have experienced it. Indeed, even though I went through the traumatic reality of a near-death experience and suffered the aftermath, at times I still find it hard to comprehend how a car accident that one lived through could be so devastating and life changing. I am pleased to say, I am now able to own the experience and slowly but surely reveal the gems within it. Strange as it might seem, the car accident has been a pivotal point in my discovery of self and spiritual resilience. The revelation of those gems and the full impact of the road traffic accident are for another chapter. I now want to fast forward to a particular part in the healing process that has enabled me to be here writing this book now. The catalyst in this aspect of the healing process began when I decided to trust to the Most High and attempt to get on a plane to Ghana.

# Chapter 19

## Dear Yahweh

While in conversation with the most high I asked a question. How one can become closer to spirit and how I can help spirit. This was the answer I received.

"Trust what you hear and know that I am talking to you for the first time. A time has come for you to listen. it is for the greater good of all. Read what you have written about spirit and hear THE INNER MESSAGE.

"I want to reach all the souls of the inner planes and need to do this for the greater good of all. Trust what you get, feel the feelings of trust, and know that you are guided by them. Hold on to the love you have in your heart. You have shown that you can be compassionate—I now need you to be forceful and intolerant of the pain you witness around you. Take whatever action you can to relieve others of pain. Do the healing work you have been blessed to do. Take this matter seriously and reach out to people. Offer to heal and know that it will be done. Do not worry about the cost or the bills—this is a minor matter in comparison to the desperate work that is needed to heal the world.

"I require an open mind and a willing heart, without fear or reservation. I will express pure love for all and through all.

"The angels are with you. Trust them, embrace them and allow them to advise you. Take instruction and guidance. Give of your wisdom. Yes, you are the oracle of the day, as are many others. Use this gift wisely and know that we listen and hear all that is said. Remember, integrity is not about me or you but about the respect and care of the other person. If you hold in mind that these are precious beings that you are dealing with, you will never go wrong. Do not judge them by their garments or their words but by the feelings they give off. Listen to their very hearts and hear them speak for the first time. Connect with their trust and truth and they will see in you the reflection of the divine.

"To assist spirit, you must be spirit—you must know that your face, purse or ability is not the significant matter. Be the pure energy that allows other energies to dwell in peace. Be the tower of strength and know it is strong because it can stand amongst all other strengths with no desire to crush or inhibit them. Be young at heart and old in mind so that wisdom and knowledge can flow through you easily. Be like the curious child and the careful old woman. Be like the wise old man and the mischievous boy all at the same time and be the unbounded energy of joy, bliss, experience and acceptance. Be love in its fullest form, just being love. When a loving feeling surges through your body from the pit of your kundalini (a form of divine energy located in the lower part of the body) to your sahasrara (the crown of your seventh chakra at the top of the head), know that I am with you and ready to express, in whatever way is needed.

"I feel your pain tenfold and I know your struggle, but what you fail to see is that you are struggling in your sleep, fighting no one but yourself and you wonder why you cannot win this battle or end this ordeal. You need to wake up and realise that there is no struggle, only expressions of feelings and lack of feelings. Choose to be blissful instead. That is all you need to do. Oh, please know that I am not negating your pain, just your perception of it.

"Love me without intention of gain and you will gain everything and need nothing. Trust me without wavering and you will banish fear. Respect me above all others and you will have but one master. Keep me close like a precious memory and no other thoughts will distress you. I am more powerful than words can express, but I am not controlling, so the choice is yours or that of whoever you have given the power of mastery to.

"Don't worry so much about your thoughts, think more on the actions you failed to take and know that they have consequences too. Not only the lack of results that these actions might have brought, but more importantly the negative seeds that unfulfilled actions bear. In other words, if trees are not planted in your garden you will never know the pleasure of new leaves. I am talking about life and changing experiences. I mean the things that cause things to be different may be more about what you fail to start rather than what you failed to finish. You have a saying about missing one's calling; I would say waiting to be called is the mistake. There is a part of you that knows all that you can be doing and another part of you that waits for someone outside of yourself to recognise this and call it to your attention. What if they never speak of it? Will you pretend you don't know it, or will you deem it to be unworthy of action?

"Know that I am going to love you whatever you do, or whatever you don't do. My love for you is unconditional. The real question is: what do you need to do or not do, in order to love yourself? The answer to this question is the purpose of life, and only you have the answers. This is the gift I have given you and the challenge you choose to take. The journey through life is not a game, nor should it be a struggle. It is, in fact, a necessary path to that amazing and overwhelming powerful feeling that your inner soul has a memory of and your mind has forgotten, or at least avoided remembering. I have not forgotten the beauty and immenseness that you really are, so I protect you and I guide you, even when you have not asked. I enable your soul to respond to that yearning for the reality that your mind has forgotten in the hope that you will find the strength to keep seeking your true self. That is why the struggle and the worry are so painful, because you know—or a part of you knows—that there is something wonderful waiting to emerge. You might liken it to a love lost and a desire to capture it again. This image is far too menial to compare with the awesome feeling and state of being that I talk of. Allow your imagination to imagine something vaster than you have ever imagined before, something so whole and complete that there is no space for doubt pain or fear. Something fully and completely packed with absolute love, something commonly known as you.

"Take heed, help is at hand in many different forms, but you must stop comparing your thoughts with that of others. Their thoughts are for them and yours are for you. I have sent angels and ancestors to whisper to you, in a tone and language that only you can hear and only you can answer to. Listen deep within the depths of you and know that the voice you may think is your own is in fact my very own messenger communicating with you. When words fail, the guides attempt skilful action to get your attention. Synchronicity is one such simple action. How many times have you said to a friend, 'I was just thinking that.' or 'how did you know that was the one I wanted?' Spirit is gently reminding you to be conscious of a presence greater than yet connected to you.

"Your spiritual gifts are so profound, you need to do nothing but be yourself. People will heal in your midst, not due to your skill but due to your ability to hold a space for God that they can step into in their time of need. Trust that I am greater than you can ever imagine. That's what the words 'to fear God' mean. Know that I will hold your hand just as long as you are holding mine and, at the same time, I will hold so many other hands. Reach within yourself to find the answers and the comfort. I am waiting for you there.

# Chapter 20

# Inspirational Spiritual Talk

## PRAYER- The Hidden Blessing.

This is a prayer that was created as part of my training in the two year Interfaith Seminary course that I completed, that allows me to perform, baby blessings, wedding blessings, funeral services and house blessing.

I share this with you as a way of understanding how prayer can be used in the course of individual growth and understanding.

I used this prayer in a session of Empowerment with a small group of women.

The session would open with prayers and or song, then the service would consist of something like this:

I have come to talk about hidden blessings, the type we do not notice, the type we take for granted. I am talking about the smile that a baby gives and the fact that we are able to see it, or at least sense it if we are not blessed with sight.

Sometimes life appears to be a burden and we wonder *why me*? It's a good question to ask, but we really should not be too narrow with the answers. Another good question to ask is, "Does God really think I have the strength to deal with this?" You see by asking the second question, we open the door to a spiritual answer. We bring God back into our minds and open ourselves up to the flow of his grace. Just by remembering that

God is real. What does it mean to say God is real? I have spent a lifetime trying to answer this question and many things in life have evidenced to me that the existence of the Most High is truly real. Sometimes I ask for things that I do not get, but when I consider what has happened instead it is often a better result in the long term. I guess that is what having faith is all about, the skill of trusting that the Most High really does have your back and knows how to meet your needs even better than you. This is not easy, I know, but I have learned that it's better than suffering alone.

You see, when you open up to the presence of God in your life, you are no longer saying 'I have got to do this alone'. You are actually saying, 'When the weight gets too heavy, please carry it for me'.

Children, very little children, have the right idea. Do you think most small children will wait until they are tired before they ask to be carried? No, their logic is, 'Mum you have the strength. Dad you've got the muscles. Don't let me get tired, just lift me up now because you don't want to see me suffer, do you?'

We should be the same with our God—'Dear Lord you know what is before me, you know how to meet my needs, so support me now before I struggle because I know you love me and have no desire to see me suffer.'

It's not about giving up your independence or being big enough to stand on your own two feet. It is about acknowledging that there is more to you than you might recognise and that you have other skills and tools at your disposal. In other words, you have support over and above your physical being, however, you need to know how to access it. This is where being grown up and independent comes in. You see, as a child you knew or maybe had a sense that there was something greater to explore, that you might have abilities that you had not discovered yet then you got to adolescence and forgot. We start to believe that all we have is what we can taste, see, smell, touch and hear. We stop exploring, we stop believing and we give up on discovering other aspects of ourselves.

Soon after this stage, society kicks in and tells us loud and clear that we are separate from all others and the only way to make it, is to make it on your own. Hence, we start the process of suffering alone. Sometimes we even feel good about that. How often have you heard people say, 'and I managed it all by myself!' and we respond by saying that's good. In fact, what it is in reality is very sad. It's sad that we are not making use of a loving and devoted Almighty who has offered his service without compromise or condition and not acknowledging the presence of this force in our life to ask for what we want.

Any good manager will tell you that the art of good management is not to do it all by yourself but to delegate and give clear instructions. Praying holds the same principles, with a slight difference. In prayer we do delegate and hand it over to God and we give clear instructions as to what we want. However, in the case of praying to the Most High, we need to remember that God is the manager and therefore is wiser, so we leave the *how it is done* to God and, unlike the business manager, we don't need to check that it is done. All we have to do is trust because God is happy to work with us and through us, if only we would let him.

We have the ability to access a wonderful source, but in order to do it we need to change our mindset and open our hearts to loving help, which may come in many different guises.

My grandson has a habit of saying, "I want food and I want it now." In that small phrase, there is clear instruction, clear delegation and absolute expectation. We should pray in this way, knowing that we are children of the Most High.

# Chapter 21

## Let It Be So and So It Is

Let it be so. How often have we struggled with a decision to be made or a choice that feels like we really have no options. After hours of thought and ideas rushing back and forth in our minds, we decide to give up on the decision we really want to make and choose the alternative. Oh sure, we give ourselves logical, moral and financial explanations for our un-chosen option, but at the end of the day it is we, within our own minds, that decide to let it be so. Hence, we start the creation followed by the manifestation of the very things we don't really want in our lives. It is usually at the manifestation stage, which is often far too late, that we realise, this is not the outcome we desired. So where in our God-given creative process did we fail? The truth is we did not fail, we just offered ourselves another opportunity to learn more about the limited or expanded use of our thoughts and actions.

Many have written about the power of thought and the ability to visualize and create what one wants in their lives. Authors such as Napoleon Hill, Louise Hay, Shakti Gawain and Deepak Chopra, to mention a few, all offer guidelines and instructions as to how to use your God-given creative thought pattern to improve your health, wealth and spiritual attributes. All the books by the aforementioned authors are well worth reading. I have found the above authors to be exceptionally inspiring, but there comes a time when all the books in the world will be of no use to you unless you master the art of managing the 'let it be so syndrome'. What I am really talking about is the type of seeds that we plant in the garden of our minds.

Let's imagine that within us there is an amazing void of dark empty space and every thought is a flash of light. As those lights come shooting through the dark empty spaces, they leave particles, like memory dust, that fall to the foundation of the empty void and embed themselves there. However, these particles can do nothing until more similar particles fall on top of them, at which point they are no longer dust like, but are tall and prominent with a wealth of light. At which point there are enough light particles—or rather the light of thought particles—that they are now able to shine brightly and glow, just like the original thought—because they are now rooted in the void, which is no longer empty as it consists of those bright thought particles and the more the particles fall on top of the others in the void, the more they are instantly attracted to their counterparts, or similar forms, then the roots grow stronger, until they are able to branch out further into the void, emanating a light that mirrors the original Idea or thought that is now more powerful and ready to create. The process continues, when finally the void fears that it is at risk of overrunning the void. After all, all the void wants to do is to be in its stillness. When all the tranquillity is lost in the void and the space is now bright with thought particles, the void decides that it can no longer contain the volume of this particular thought branch and its very strong roots and must release it or be rid of it in order to resume its original state of deep dark non-activity. It is as if the void says, "This is not my stuff or issue, I do not desire this thought and I no longer want it in my space. This is your stuff so manage it in your space, the material world." Void uses its power of transformation to eject the thought particles, roots and branches included, and sends it flying into the world we know as reality. In fact, our outer world, perceived as divided from thought, is probably just another void of a different type, which may have a different task than the void of our inner self.

# Chapter 22

## Spiritually Touching the Lives of Others

Human beings are not separate entities who live in their own heads or can survive through their own endeavours. We need each other to bounce ideas off or at least to have someone acknowledge that we are here and have views, feelings and intentions. Nothing is more rewarding than to speak to someone who has great insight into the fact that you exist, have a personal history and are striving for more. When managed with integrity and genius, the art of mediumship or clairvoyance meets this need well for some people.

I have had the privilege, and it is a privilege, of joining with others to explore their life experiences, as well as connecting with those in spirit who are also deeply concerned for the individual's past, current and future affairs.

For as long as I can remember, I have always been acutely aware of what people are really feeling and could often tap into that emotion and feel it myself. I learnt to detach my own feelings from this and just be an observer of this phenomena. I then discovered that if I get close to the person in my mind and try to see more of what is behind their current mood or persona, amazing things happen. I find my mind flooded with information as to why they are feeling the way they do, and I see pictures of events that have happened in their lives previously. If I remain relaxed and focused, I am then able to pick up on images and words from others, alive or dead, who are interested in the person in question. This ability always amazes me, and I have tried long and hard to find a logical explanation as to how this can happen, but without success. Yet time and time again, I meet people and they allow me to touch their lives and be party to another realm connected to them. In return, I listen intently to them and share feelings of absolute honesty and true positive regard.

Even though, as a child, I would tell family members what I could see happening in their lives or a dream that revealed events that might unfold, this only happened when it wanted to. I could not tell if and when an insight would come to me. I therefore accepted it as something that just happened from time to time. I perceived this as just another bodily function like the ability to see, smell or hear. In fact, it was more like those tiny glittery stars that you sometimes see in front of your eyes that you know do not really exist but appear for some reason and then just go away by themselves. It was only when I attended a Louise Hay Workshop in Birmingham called *Love Yourself Heal Your Life* that I became aware of the fact that I could connect with the lives of others and communicate with spirit as a planned process.

I recall being in a very large group of people, mainly women, and that the workshop left some people in tears while others were jubilant. All were keen to resolve inner conflict and pain or at least find themselves in a place where they could feel more at home with themselves. I had decided to stay with Aunt May before attending the four-day residential workshop. As usual, Aunt May and Uncle Dave simply accepted that I was doing something to further my education and develop my skills. Indeed, I was not totally sure why I was attending, all I knew was the workshop offered me an opportunity to meet others who were interested in understanding themselves better and resolving some internal unanswered questions.

My dear Uncle Dave made sure that I knew where I was going and ordered the taxi in time for me to set out early. On arrival, I entered a huge dark red brick building. It looked like a college, but there were no students about. The building was in a quiet part of Birmingham, where I had not been before. I arrived with my bags and usual jolly self, keen to meet others. Of course, as usual, I expected to be the only black person there and, indeed, I was, but there was also a Spanish woman there and others who had travelled from Scotland, Ireland and other parts of the world to be there, which meant I was quite at home with my very English accent and London knowledge. The group consisted of about forty people.

We all entered a large hall and sat in a very big circle and, without much talk, we very quickly got into the work of appreciating and accepting each other, then meditating. I sat next to a White woman who looked about fifty years old, had a plump round face and short curly brown hair with grey streaks. She was very nervous and quite critical of the fact that there were so many people in the room—"How are they going to manage such a large group?" she whispered to me. I realised that a part of her needed to rubbish the process in case she did not get what she wanted. We continued to talk, but I found her attitude to be very negative and wondered if I was also feeling fearful or negative and if that was the reason why she found it so easy to talk to me about her damning views. The next day I sat away from her but kept an eye on her because I was very concerned as to how she was doing. She, in fact, did OK and got the support she required despite of the large numbers.

I had decided to take this as a serious retreat for my mind and body as well as spirit, so I would exercise every morning, just a few stretches and sit-ups for about ten minutes. Then I would flick the Bible open and read any passage that I opened to and I would pray and ask for guidance in order to receive what was required for me during this experience. After that was one, I would face the day in my usual joyous fashion, ready to accept all that might happen.

The *Love Yourself Heal Your Life* workshop went well, and I was now on the penultimate day, by which time we had all got to know each other a little better and had shared some personal detail+ of our lives. During the lunch break, a young woman approached me and said, "Aqualma, you seem to be in tune with spirit—do you think you could give me a reading?" I responded by asking her, "What is a reading?" She explained that a reading is doing what I did for my family when they asked for spiritual guidance. I explained that I don't do that. I only tell people what I feel, if and when I feel it. She was, however, persistent and encouraged me to try. I made no promises. We sat down and I held her hand, then told her I could not see or feel anything. She seemed shocked and asked me to keep trying.

At this time, I felt this was wrong, almost as though I was attempting to force God to communicate with us, when God just was not ready to do that. I explained this to the woman and said, maybe we should try this later. She was disappointed but keen to try later. As she took her small brown bag of fruits and walked out into the large well-groomed gardens of the red brick building, I wondered about the possibility of calling on the spirits and God at any other time outside of when I know that they are connecting with me. In that moment I decided to give the woman a reading. As I held her hand and closed my eyes, I asked spirit, to help me. I took a deep breath and then I saw a large man with a leather belt, strapped round his bear belly like stomach. I then saw what appeared to be his under pants, in bright colours, reds, yellows and blues. then I became aware of an image of the cartoon characters, Minnie mouse and Mickey mouse. I then let go of the woman's hands, apologised to her and explained what I had seen in my mind's eye. I told her of the big belly man and the leather belt surrounding his large stomach and the image of the Mickey mouse characters that I saw. At which point the woman said, 'oh my God, that is my husband, and his does have a large stomach, yet more surprisingly I bought him some under pants recently which were bright in colour and have Mickey and Minnie mouse on printed on them. I knew in that moment that my future would be to take this gift of seeing the lives of others and use it for the greater good of all.

# Chapter 23

## Positive Thinking Programme - (created and designed by Aqualma Empowerment Services)

This task-focused work will assist you to understand what you are experiencing and will enable you to adjust negative thoughts and feelings.

You will require, pen/pencil and paper. You may choose to keep what you do or throw some of it away. What you create is yours to do with as you will. It is all up to you.

The work you do here and the answers to these questions are to provide you with a private space to explore what is happening to you and to help you realise that you are able to heal yourself right now and feel better in yourself.

Work at your own pace. You can share what you do with others, but only if you want to.

Any thing you do, or any answers you give, are fine and will be just what you need to be doing in order to heal quickly. Trust yourself and know that you are guided.

There are no wrong or right answers. Your experience and what you feel are valuable and worthy of expression.

You may choose to read this over and over again and then, when you are ready, you will start to feel better and will find the questions easy to understand and answer.

As you work through the questions and tasks you may, if you choose, sense a feeling of safety and comfort which will bring about peacefulness and sometimes happiness will be experienced.

I suggest you answer the questions in the order presented, but feel free to follow your spirit and do what feels right for you.

Try not to think too long or hard about what to say or do, just write down what comes to you easily and naturally.

Now the journey from where you are right now to where you can be, begins.

1. Right now, I feel…
2. Right now, I think…
3. What I would change if I could is…
4. What I would want not to change is…
5. The three times in my life when I was really content and happy were…
6. If I could turn back the clock, what I would change is… and the new outcome would be…
7. My greatest achievement in life thus far is… and I remember feeling…

Draw an outline of your body, then draw something that describes the pain in your body.

Draw this symbol on the part of the body where you feel the pain.

If you could speak to the pain in your body what would you say to it now? Write or draw your answer here (or you may wish to do it on a different sheet).

Imagine your pain is an enemy. What might be its motive for attacking you?

Imagine your pain is a friend. What might be its motives for causing you to feel this way?

Is your pain here to help you or to hurt you?

If you had a switch to turn off your pain, what would you miss most about it?

How would your life be different without the pain?

Recall a time in your life when you helped someone. Tell the story here.

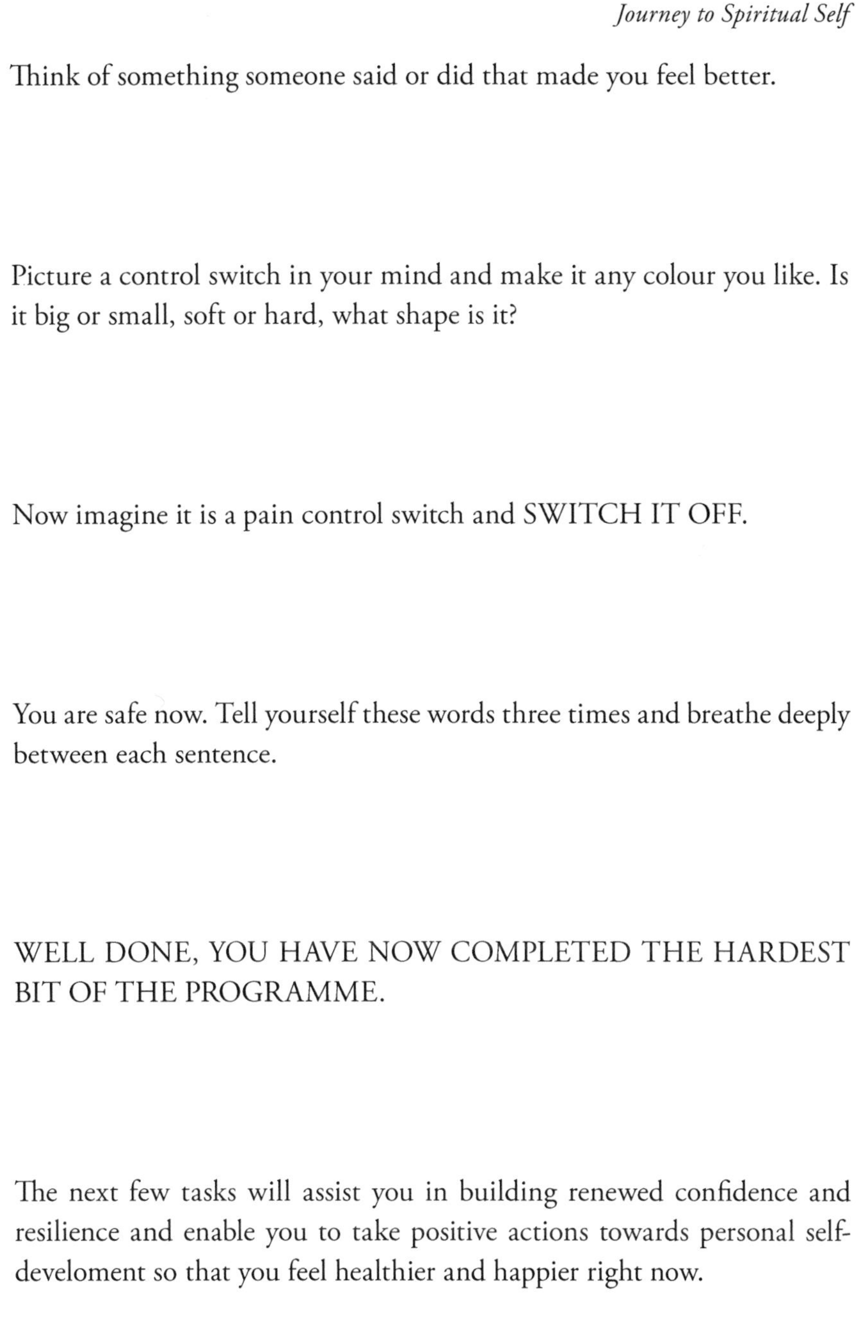

Think of something someone said or did that made you feel better.

Picture a control switch in your mind and make it any colour you like. Is it big or small, soft or hard, what shape is it?

Now imagine it is a pain control switch and SWITCH IT OFF.

You are safe now. Tell yourself these words three times and breathe deeply between each sentence.

WELL DONE, YOU HAVE NOW COMPLETED THE HARDEST BIT OF THE PROGRAMME.

The next few tasks will assist you in building renewed confidence and resilience and enable you to take positive actions towards personal self-develoment so that you feel healthier and happier right now.

For the next 24 hours keep all that you are feeling and thinking about to yourself, you are safe now and it is ok to feel what you are feeling within yourself, as you are internally secure now. They say if you count your blessings, then you open the way for more blessings to emerge, so make a list of all the things you are grateful for, no matter how small or simple. Start with something like I am really grateful for breathing, for water, and being able to know that I am alive, etc.

For the next twenty-one nights or days, copy down the following positive statements. You can add your own but do keep them simple and avoid the use of negative words. Even though these statements may not feel true at this time, you are in the process of clearing your mind of negative thoughts in order to bring about peace of mind and better emotional, physical and mental health. The affirmations below will support your mind in getting rid of negative thoughts and replace them with positive ones. Twenty-one days should do it. You can write them out as often as you like. When the twenty-one days are over, place a copy of the words below in a place where you will see them every day (like the bathroom mirror) and know that you are healed.

- *I am protected and safe now and always.*
- *I am healthy, strong and thriving.*
- *All that I require I have.*
- *I am happy content and supported.*
- *I have love, joy and peace.*
- *I am prosperous and abundant.*
- *I am relaxed calm and comfortable.*

*This is true now and always.*

*This or something better manifests in my life and so it is, and it is so.*

*Give thanks (here you may add something if you are spiritual or religious utilising the name you use for praising the Most High, otherwise you can give thanks for being)*

CONGRATULATIONS! YOU HAVE TAKEN GREAT STEPS TOWARDS A WHOLE AND COMPLETE YOU.

# Chapter 24

## Contemplating Relationships

Intimacy and meaningful relationships are often spoken about in terms of making it work or understanding the other. In reality deep, potentially loving relationships often consist of intensive thinking and hypothesising about what the other person is like, what they will do or if they will be there tomorrow. My thoughts when in romantic entanglement are extremely complex and I have learned that in relationships it is feelings that should be trusted not logical thoughts, as love guides the heart and not logic. Trust your spirit to guide you when thinking about intimate relationships. There is no sense to it, just feeling, and if it feels right go with it, remembering to respect yourself and others in the process.

Dear Lord

I pray to you today and ask that you kindly take from me the defences that I choose to give up at this time. I know you appreciate how hard this is for me Lord, and that you will help me in every way you can. I understand that I must take some action to seal my commitment to change and letting go. The action I take right now is to trust you Lord and to allow myself to think in new and courageous ways. Here we go.

Dear Lord,

Today I choose to give up the defence of untidiness. It helped me to appear less capable, so that others made fewer demands on me. It also provided me with a good excuse to keep people out of my life, as I could pretend that I did not want them to see what a mess I was in. I am ready to give up the internal and external mess now, Lord, and be all the wonderful things I really am. I am ready to risk getting close to others and to trust that they won't hurt me or make me dirty in any way. I am ready to stop pretending to myself and be all that I am. I choose to give up the defence of professionalism, as I hide behind the fact that I am this informed, disciplined, righteous professional who has to conduct myself in this way at all times because my job seems more like a way of life than work. Law and order has been my whole persona. It gives me an air of importance and protects me from people who may choose to get close. They end up feeling intimidated, judged, and they withdraw. I now choose to be Aqualma, sometimes right sometimes wrong, sensitive, accepting and spiritual. I choose to be respected, valued and loved for who I am not what I am.

I choose to give up the defence of chaos, which has assisted me in not committing to many things and given me an excuse for my failings, or rather not pursuing my potential successes. Today I embrace my ability to succeed and my skill in managing difficult situations, without crediting my achievements to luck. Today I accept that I am working in partnership with God and that I am capable of being a more useful and productive partner for the greater good of myself and others.

I choose to let go of the defence of fear, which manifests in my life as over-cautiousness, being controlling, not taking suitable risks, limiting my ambitions and acting impulsively in inappropriate situations. I will, as of now, acknowledge my fear and choose to trust in my inner wisdom and God to guide and keep me safe. I will remember that the past was a dangerous and painful place, but this is now history and today I only attract good things and people into my life. I will remind myself that God has great plans for me and only desires that I grow, achieve and embrace all aspects of love, abundance, peace and joy.

I let go of the defence of believing in self-destruction. I know that a part of me thinks that if anybody is going to destroy me, I would rather that person was me, so I do all sorts of things to sabotage myself, in terms of planning preparation and sometimes lack of confidence. Inadvertently, I give away my power and set others up to hurt and destroy me in some way. As of today, I let go of the need to be self-destructive by proxy or in any other form. I will love and protect myself in every way I can. I accept that I am here to live and not be destroyed, and that my task is not only to survive but also to grow through all my experiences. I will utilise my spirituality not as a shield but as a wonderful tool to enrich my life and the life of others.

For this insight, I thank you, Lord. Please help me to gain more understanding and knowledge so that I can be all that you intended me to be. Please replace all the above defences with love and any other ingredient you know I need so that I will be nourished and equipped to do your work successfully.

In you, Lord, is my trust and gratitude. I know from this moment on, my life will be very different.

Thank You.
Love Aqualma S.Y. Murray.

# Chapter 25

## "Life Plans"

Sometimes in life we feel lost and confused as to our path forward. This often happens at stages in our lives when we have completed elements of our life plans. The thing about life plans is that we make them in our teens or even earlier. We often take steps to fulfil that which may change on the way to completion, however, we stick to them in some way, either by saying 'this is who I am' or 'this is what I want or need to do'. Then somewhere down the road, we forget what the original plan was, as we are often forced to change course or accommodate situations. We plod on and find ourselves doing things we are not conscious of choosing.

You see, at the age of twelve or thirteen, we often decide who we are going to be. You remember it is at that stage we say things like 'I am never going to allow anyone to fool me again' or 'I have decided that I am going to see the world', or 'from this day forth I will never lie again'. Whatever we decide, we often stick to the script that we choose. I recall deciding that I would never play second fiddle to any man, and that I would always do just what I wanted to, no matter who didn't like it. I decided I was going to be nice to people because I realised that life is not easy and is only made more difficult by people who are not nice to each other. Well, sticking to those decisions has brought me joy and pain at different times in my experience. The problem was that I forgot what I chose, so could not appreciate just how and why I did the things I did, when ultimately it was not in my best interest in many situations.

However, it is through making such life choices and experiencing the consequences that we learn so much about ourselves, if, and only if, we are wise and astute enough to remember who we were and be conscious of who we are becoming. That is the skill in managing life changes—to hold on to the lessons from our past and bring the learning from those experiences into our future. Therein lies the ability to transform gracefully and responsibly with an appreciation of knowing how we came to be. Such knowledge allows us to be humble and tolerant of the journey of others as we recall the path that got us to where we are and remember that we have not always stuck to our task or responded as we would have liked, due to the pressure and trials of our daily experiences. It is true, however, that you can make positive use of all that happens to you and be wise enough to know that every experience, no matter how negative it might seem, is ultimately a blessing because it has propelled you into a new understanding and a better method of managing and coping with future realities in your life and the lives of others that you care about.

It is through evaluating and re-evaluating what we want to achieve and remembering our reasons for our choices that we grow and develop with a sense of confidence and resilience. If, however, we allow our decisions to chop and change or follow the ideas of others without any regard as to why we chose the paths that we attempted to follow, then we end up lost, confused and bewildered as to what we want to do, where our strengths lie and how we can go forward. You see, without recollection of the past and how it has brought us to where we are, we have no foundation. And it is true a tree without roots is simply standing there and rotting before our very eyes. That is the reality of many people's lives. Is it any wonder that so many are bitter and unloving and others are so disregarding of the lives and wellbeing of their fellow man, woman and child? We need to remember who we are and where we are coming from in order to master our future and progress with planned flexibility and adaptation, when moving strategically from our original plan. It is ok to change your mind and move on, but never forget the reasons why you are making new decisions today compared with the decisions of yesterday. To forget is to risk reproducing a past that you have already experienced. Hopefully should have learned lessons from that past that will enable you to go forward armed with new skills and knowledge.

Despite what we have decided for ourselves many years ago, we have the power and the ability to change it now. As stated by Louise Hay, in her book that sold nearly one million copies, *You Can Heal Your Life*, we need to know that we have the capacity to change our lives right now in this very moment. "The point of Power is always in the present moment. You are never stuck. This is where the changes take place, right here and right now in our minds! It doesn't matter how long we've had a negative pattern or an illness or a poor relationship or a lack of finances or self-hatred. We can begin to make a shift today!" (Ch 4. p36).

The way to make a shift in our lives is to really think about the things we want to manifest in our life. If I decide that I want to lose weight, then I consciously imagine myself shopping for smaller clothes, feeling thinner and looking more like the shape that I want. Then I start to train my mind to believe this by repeating positive words in my head, and out loud, I say, "I am shaped beautifully, I wear a comfortable size twelve and I look great all the time, I am healthy and happy in my body." I then add that this or something better should manifest in my life, and the reason I do this is because I do not know what the future holds for me and it may be this extra weight that I have attracts my future soul mate. Thus, in order not to close the door on my future blessings, I allow the Most High to decide what is best for me. These things I have learnt on my path of spirituality through reading many books by authors such as Louise Hay, Shakti Gawain, Coraline Myss and many others (please see bibliography at the end of the book).

As you attempt to change yourself, it is important to love yourself throughout the process. For example, if you have a health condition that you would like to change, you must not hate that condition or reject it but rather ask yourself, what lessons can I learn from this condition and what have I learnt from the experience, then thank the condition for the experience and tell yourself you are now ready to let it go, with love and gratitude rather than fear, anger or hatred.

For example, if you had a disfiguring skin condition you may have learnt what it is like to be different from others, you may have suffered discomfort, the condition may have forced you to find other qualities in yourself other than physical ones. It is important to acknowledge these lessons and embrace them as coping methods that you have now mastered and be ready to let go of them in order to experience something new.

Only then can a positive change take place. I know that this is not easy, especially if you have suffered due to your condition and this has had a very negative impact on your life thus far. Remember, change is possible and a new day can come. Now you will benefit from seeing yourself anew, doing the things you could not do before and imagining yourself without the previous condition. Picture the new you as often as you can and say the affirming words that remind you to believe that things are different now, such as 'my skin is smooth and beautiful and I have restful nights without any pain or irritation'. Alternatively, you may be affirming that you have healthy lungs and no longer cough uncontrollably. You need to hold a positive thought and a joyous state of mind as you affirm these things, for it is not only your words that bring about the change but also your deepest thoughts and beliefs.

Some twenty-five years ago, I recall an experience that left me very confused and scared. I found myself losing my temper uncontrollably. On one occasion I was asked by a bus conductor to pay an extra fifty pence on my fare. At that point, I became quite irate and started to curse the man. When his manager appeared, I cursed him too. I told them two bad words that I find hard to repeat on these pages, and, as I walked away from them, I could hear myself cursing them at the top of my voice.

This was very out of character for me and I became worried that I might be losing my mind, so I went to the doctor and said, "I am very stressed, I am losing my temper and find it hard to control my anger. I get hot and sweaty easily and I have trouble sleeping. I think I need help as I am losing my mind."

The doctor said he would like to do some tests and took some blood. On my return to the surgery, he was pleased to tell me that he had found the source of my problem and announced that I had an over-active thyroid that was causing my mood swings and irritation along with my sleep and skin problems. He treated my condition with medication and said that if that didn't work I might need an operation. A year later my thyroid was still unstable, sometimes too high and other times too low. I was losing weight rapidly and on other occasions gaining it very quickly. The doctors decided that I needed an operation. They offered me an opportunity to drink a dose of radioactive solution that would poison my system for up to three months. I decided against that, so the other option was to have my throat cut. I went for the latter.

After spending six days in hospital and having several surgical staples in my neck, I was allowed to go home. The doctors had to cut out most of my thyroid gland in order to correct my condition. After surgery, it was explained to me that my thyroid was now unable to work by itself and that I would need to take medication for the rest of my life. This medication would mean that I would be unable to drink alcohol. This shocked me and the thought of having to take medication every day of my life and never drink brandy again was not acceptable to me. I told my doctor that I refused to take the medication and that I would pray instead. He warned me seriously and said that my health would suffer if I didn't take medication and I would be putting myself at risk. I thanked him dearly and went home.

Right away, I started praying for health and freedom from the need for medication. I began to imagine that my body was healthy and well. I asked myself, what were the lessons in this situation and decided that the lesson was something about valuing my ability to be humble and respectful to others. I also needed to appreciate how wonderful my voice and my body was. Throughout the hospital experience, I learnt a great deal about the people around me, in terms of how much they loved and cared for me, as well as learning about those who loved me, but could not support me.

I started to state affirmations every day: 'my body is whole complete and perfect and my thyroid works well and supports me'. I would imagine little people going inside me and planting new thyroid glands. They would tend it like it was a precious garden and would look after the inside of me. Some six months later, I attended the hospital for a regular check, and they said my thyroid was struggling to work, but doing ok. Six months later, the doctor told me that my thyroid had grown back and was working normally. It continues to do so and the only time I have problems is when I am very stressed or run down. At those times, my thyroid suffers most and does not function as well as it can, but indeed it is there and has grown back to a normal healthy size. My thyroid continued to work for some twenty years without any medication, however, as I have grown older and experienced more stress, my body has needed a little help, so I now take a very small amount of Thyroxin per day to keep my recovered thyroid in check. By the grace of the Most High my body healed itself—and yours can do the same.

# Chapter 26

## Each One Teach One: Raising a Positive Black Male Child (Against all the Odds)

I was blessed with just one pregnancy and one boy child, as the Lord knew what I could manage and gave me no more than that. The Most High had a plan and set me a task to see if, given the choice and the option, I could really give a child the opportunity to have a growing experience that would equip him for future life and allow him to have a fruitful and enjoyable childhood, in spite of all the odds.

I am proud to say that my baby is now twenty-eight years old and anyone who knows him and has the pleasure of relating to him finds it compelling to tell me what a fine young man he is. Little do they know just how fine he is, for they only see the surface, outer vision of him. Some get to experience the service of how wonderful, committed, dedicated, honouring and loyal this child is to all that he believes.

When I was pregnant at the age of nineteen, all I desired was a cute little dark-skinned boy, who would grow to be tall and handsome. I did not think of his character, future or qualities, except to wish that he had manners and could be someone that I could converse with. If the truth be known, I had my baby at a time in my life when I felt life was not worth living and my existence was meaningless, so I needed a reason to live and having a child was it. I desired to have an opportunity to raise a child in a right and correct fashion, in a way that would allow that child to thrive and manage all the ups and downs he would be bound to face. I wanted to teach him all that I knew and afford him an opportunity to learn all that I could not, for his sake.

The moment he was born and I looked at him I realised—suddenly it dawned on me—that this child was not here to fulfil my wishes but rather we were placed together to assist each other in the next avenues of our journey. The task was to grow, survive and thrive together. This for me was a great revelation as I became aware that not only was I here to feed and nurture, but I also had to be all that I was, if I wished to be in a position to model the skills of surviving, thriving and succeeding to my sweet little child.

PJ and I relaxing in the park 1984

The Most High had kept his end of the bargain, indeed I had a cute, dark-skinned, handsome little boy, who was all that I had imagined and more. I could see in his eyes that he came prepared to be guided by me and I had no choice but to attempt to do this to the best of my ability. However, I had just turned twenty years old and did not have a clue. All I knew was that it was important to be honest to my child and to trust that he would be able to cope with all that was real. Yet I had to protect him from many things he did not need to know whilst all the time bearing in mind that he needed to be prepared, as anything could happen. My traumatic life experience had taught me that anything could happen, in spite of your parents' very good intentions and I had to ensure that my boy was strong enough and ready on many different levels; in particular emotionally, intellectually, morally and spiritually. The reflection of how this was successfully achieved is a story of utilising all that I had known, trusting all that I was guided to say and do with my child, and taking some risks which were outside of my knowing.

My son is now a strong, physically attractive, well-focused, disciplined, honouring and morally sound young man. In his presence, you can feel an energy of sureness and humble acceptance of all that is around him, yet an intolerance of anything that is not wholesome, God-loving or respectful to others. He is ambitious yet grounded in what is real and possible. He is patient and deeply understanding of many of the dynamics about him with a clear sense of what he should attempt to change and what he should allow to be or what it is necessary to let go of. He is able to manage life's challenges with deep feeling and consideration. I am sure he does not find any of this totally easy, but he is confident that he has the tools to achieve all that he desires and to assist others along the way. Most amazingly, he has managed to embrace a relationship with the Most High God in a manner that goes beyond any aspect of the spiritual understanding that I attempted to impart to him. He has a closeness to God that allows for an easy and valuing acceptance of all the principles of the universe that he has managed to internalise in a way that affords him deep intimacy with the Most High and great value for all that God gives him. Indeed, he often reminds me of many wonderful aspects of the Most High that I have forgotten during hard times. Hence, the coming together of two souls my son and mine, destined to thrive or fail, depending on how well we utilise this life's opportunity to excel to the next level.

I want to talk to you about how my son and I came to be who we are today and the powerful spiritual experiences throughout our journey to self and being who we are in life.

My son often reminds me of things I have told him, and the words of wisdom I have shared with him. I am usually amazed and in awe of the things he feeds back to me. The other day he told me that I told him to trust in himself and the only way to make real changes is to change oneself, then others will have to adapt. It is no use trying to change others. When he told me this, I knew I agreed with it but could not imagine that I would have told my teenage son this and even more that he would have remembered it and lived his life by it. We are very powerful as parents and need to remember that our children believe what we tell them, even if *we* really don't. I am pleased that I was in a place where I could give my son the right guidance and support, as it is also true to say that that skill and ability was a fleeting moment of clarity that I must have had and I thank the Most High I was able to share with him.

So now that I am not in such a positive place, PJ, at the age of thirty seven, is able to remind me of the faith, trust and hope I had in the Most High and also the ability to trust oneself and not try to change others but just work on oneself. This is what this book is all about—making changes in life by working on you. The moment that you trust that you can, then amazing things happen. I am learning yet again to trust in the Most High. As experiences have shaken my trust and left me wondering, the Most High has allowed my son to remember the positive teaching, and now he is re-educating me, with the very wisdom that I taught him. It makes me wonder at just how great the Most High is.

I believe nothing is by chance and that the universe has plotted a path for us that is not fixed but skilfully designed to meet all our needs while allowing us free will. How great is that? I think it is far beyond great and a more intrinsically planned way than we of mortal existence could ever imagine. How blessed are we?! All praises be to the Most High.

My message to all parents out there, especially mothers raising boys by themselves, is to remember that your child is acutely aware of all that you believe and the energy you attract. Hence, it is very important that you are aware of it as well, in order to understand what you are doing and why. It is also true that our actions or lack of actions are the greatest lessons to our children. They need to see that you can meet your own needs as well as theirs and that you are able to make conscious and sensible decisions about what and who you expose them to.

It is also crucial that you monitor your emotional responses to things in the presence of your child so that they learn an element of control. Remember, children are in tune with what you are feeling, so they will know that you are making an effort to control your outward emotions and will therefore learn to manage their internal emotions as well.

Help your children to consider 'what if'. In other words, have discussions with them that allow them to see the bigger picture or the potential consequences of their actions. This teaching will enable them to think themselves into a given situation and plan an appropriate reaction. Remember, the power of thought is great and if they have pre-planted seeds (mentally) to deal with common and/or adverse situations, they will ultimately cope better if such situations arise.

While your children are young and impressionable, take the opportunity to plant positive seeds into their thoughts, such as telling them how wonderful they are, and how successful you know they can be, as my mother and brothers did for me. While your child is growing up you are the most powerful person to them. It's true that this changes when they hit the teenage years, but you have at least twelve years to plant some really significant seeds that will support and assist them during those turbulent and confusing adolescent years.

Be kind to your child and always do what's best for them, even if that means you have to be firm. Yes, we would all like to give our children all the sweets and freedom that they desire, but by placing a clear boundary around excessive behaviour we allow our children to learn something about the importance of controlling self.

As our children develop and become more independent, we have to model more trust in them and allow them to express themselves more fully. When my son became a teenager and started staying out late of an evening, I became worried for him. At that time black boys were often stopped and searched by the police and we lived in an area of some poverty, a great deal of crime and drug activity amongst young people. I thought of how I could continue to protect my child yet allow him to explore some level of freedom and independence, whilst learning to navigate the wider world. In order to help my son appreciate the concerns I had about him staying out late at night I sat with him one evening and told him that when he stayed out beyond the appointed time to return I worried that something bad might have happened to him and could not sleep until I knew he was safe. We talked about all the possible dangers of being on the streets late at night and ways to keep himself safe. I then made him a promise, that I would never embarrass him in front of his friends when he appeared to be out too late or in my mind 'missing', but he had to make me a promise in return. I asked him to promise that he would always ring me to say that he would be late and, in order not to make him look like a fool or a mummy's boy in front of his friends, he could ring me and say something like 'Hey bro, gonna be late tonight, or not going to make it tonight, see you later'. I agreed I would not question him on the phone and would address any concerns I had when he returned home. My son made the 'Hey bro' call several times and thoroughly enjoyed it as he knew I really wanted to say 'where are you, come home now' but I never did. When he did return home, I would try to stay calm and ask him why he was late, and did he remember how much I worried about him. There were occasions when I was not so calm on his return, but I stuck to my word and never humiliated or embarrassed him in front of friends. Through this experience my son learned that I respected and trusted him and he also learned to respect and trust me. To this day when we leave each other we always text or phone to say that we have reached our destination safely so that the other can sleep without worrying. Here we are teaching children and young people the art of letting go and modelling our respect for them. This is easier if we have successfully planted good positive thoughts and helped them to consider future consequences, which may come about by their actions or inactions.

Above all, teach your child to value and respect others. Simply teach them to do no harm and help others when it is safe and appropriate to do so. Remind your child that we all have our own paths and people need to be free to follow them. We can support and advise but we cannot choose the path of others, as we are only in charge of our own paths.

I recently spoke to a couple of young ladies in their late teens and early twenties. They spoke of the conflict regarding their parents in relation to their parents reuniting many years after the father left home, leaving their mother to raise them alone for the majority of their childhood. One of the girls spoke about how her mother would say the most negative things about the absent father and she, the child, felt that she had to protect and support her mother in managing the pain and loss that the father had left behind. Then, many years later, her father returned to rekindle his relationship with the mother and the child, now a young lady herself, and embarking on relationships, tried to convince her mother that this man, her father, was not a good suitor. Mum had forgotten that she had exposed the child to the pain and shame that she felt when dad left the family and could now not understand why the child was so rejecting of her plan to be with the father again. What the mother failed to recognise is that her daughter grew up experiencing her loss and saw her learning to manage without him and even get to a place where she had survived and indeed was thriving without him. If the daughter had heard a different story from the mother about the separation, such as, things changed between them or he made choices that she could not live with but that she missed him, was angry with him but did not hate him, then maybe the daughter could find a way to re-embrace him when he returned. Hence, it is important that we do not say negative things about the child's father to the child or in earshot of the child, because we may find new partners but that child will only ever have one birth father or mother. We should honour that fact and keep information appropriate at all times. I sat with the young ladies and spoke about love and commitment and how even when we know one person is not great for the other, the choice is not ours but theirs. All we can do is be there for them through the good times and the bad as they will follow their heart or mind, in spite of the wisdom we may share with them. Such teaching will help our children to manage situations without feeling responsible for others or guilt for the paths that others choose against the child's wishes.

My son and I had a distressing conversation one day when he was old enough to realise that his father only lived some five miles away yet he hardly ever saw him as his dad would visit approximately once every six months. P.J was so angry at this realisation that dad could visit but obviously did not want to and P.J said, 'That's it. I am never going to visit him either'. I said 'No son. That is not who you are, that is who your father is. I raised you to respect your elders and value your family, so in spite of your father's behaviour, you will do what you know to be right because you are a better person than that'. I then explained to my son that his father made choices. He was young and was doing the best he could, his father's best was not good or helpful to my son or to me, but it was his best. More importantly, it was his choice and we were not going to make his dad's choices impact on our behaviour because we can make our own choices based on what we know to be right or wrong. It was difficult for my son to grasp the idea that a grown man could or would not prioritise the needs of his own child, so I reminded him that some people find it difficult to consider the consequences of their actions and the possible impact it may have on others.

I am so proud of my son 'Parez-Jade Murray (P.J), he grew up and developed a positive relationship with his father. John his father had a stroke and is now a wheelchair user, so my son goes to his dad's house and cuts his hair for him. When P.J got married he invited his father to the wedding and placed him on the head table beside me, during the wedding reception John turned to me and in a lowered voice said 'Thank you for inviting me. I really was not a very good father when P.J was growing up and I am honoured to be here.' I replied, 'It's o.k., you were doing the best you could, it was not good enough for P.J and I, but it was your best.' John smiled. Then during his fatherly speech at our son's wedding he said, 'I am proud of my son and I wish I could be half the man he is.' In that moment, I was rewarded for never saying negative things to my son about his father. By remaining as positive and honest as I could, when speaking to P.J about John, a path was left open for them to find a way to a meaningful and loving relationship as father and son.

Children are extremely resilient and often prefer to know the truth, so always tell them what's true, with as much skill and sensitivity, as you can. Try your best, however, not to burden them with unnecessary truths because, after all, they expect us to manage our lives and theirs. We may need to find someone outside of the child-parent relationship to express our fears and anxieties to; this is the role of a responsible parent.

If we can do this for our children, then we free them up to follow their destiny to its natural outcome from a place of wisdom, clarity, security and love.

Having raised your child in this fashion, you can be sure you have done all you can and the Most High will do the rest. The only thing left to do is to continue developing your inner strength, for we never know when our children or other loved ones will require us to be strong for them as well as ourselves.

My dear adult son PJ, giving a wonderful, meaningful speech at the wedding of Israle and I in 2017

# Conclusion

This book has allowed the reader to consider a personal journey through the experiences of the author. We have considered the cards that are dealt to us in life and how to work with them, reject them or transform them.

The importance of positive thinking and the need to have a real and constant connection with the Most High and powerful energy life force was explored and some tools to greater connections were shared.

Through considering the inner spirit and its role in our life, we developed a greater understanding of the journey to self-empowerment.

We looked at the reality of painful life experiences and the need to build resilience, as well as spiritual muscle, to manage all that life might throw at us. We discussed the art of change and the fact that we only have the power to change ourselves, but in that change we can bring about so much change for others and the world as whole.

The experience of writing this book evidences for me that my times of adversity were not in vain and I am pleased to have shared the power in reframing negative experiences and finding the gem amongst the pain and confusion that many of us have experienced throughout childhood and our growing years. I encourage you to continue to grow and know that change can be positive no matter what has occurred in the past. You now have the power to reframe past experiences and create space for better opportunities and more fulfilling realities. Do find strength where pain and distress once dwelled and claim your happiness and success right now, for it is yours and always has been, by the grace of the Most High, loving, all powerful, universal force.

Embark on the journey to discovering more of your spiritual self, and set out at your own pace, be that with great vigour or slow contemplating serenity. Take each day as it comes and look for the lessons in every experience and encounter knowing that you are worthy and always loved. May all your relationships enhance your spiritual journey and in particular the relationship you have with yourself.

# Recommended Readers List

The Power of Positive thinking
by Norman Vincent Peale
Published -Cedar 1953 reissued 1990

The Art of Happiness A Handbook for Living
by his Holiness the Dalai Lama and Howard C.Cutler MD
Published - Hodder and Stoughton 1998

The Road Less Travelled
A New Psychology of Love, Traditional Values and Spiritual Growth
by M. Scott Peck
Published - Hutchinson and Co 1983

Further Along The Road Less Travelled The unending journey Towards Spiritual Growth
by M. Scott Peck M.D
Published -Simon and Schuster 1993

TAO The Three Treasures volume one
by BHAGWAN SHREE RAJNEESH
Published - Ma Anand Sheela 1976

Wind of the Spirit
by G.de Purucker
Published - Stockton Trade Press INC 1976

KUNDALINI And The CHAKRAS
A Practical Manual
Evolution in this lifetime
by Genevieve Lewis Paulson
Published - Llewellyn 2001

Manual Of The WARRIOR OF LIGHT
by Paulo Coelho
Published - Harper Collins 2002

African Mythology
by Geoffrey Parrinder
Published - Chancellor Press 1996

Longman Pocket English Dictionary
A first learning dictionary
by A W Frisby
Published - Longman group 1975

Conversations with God book 3
An uncommon dialogue
by Neale Donald Walsch
Published - Hodder and Stoughton 1998

Living with Joy
keys to personal Power and Spiritual Transformation
by Sanaya Roman
Published - H J Kramer 1986

The Power is Within You
by Louise L.Hay
Published - Eden Grove Editions 1991

Creative Visualization
Use The Power of Your Imagination to Create What You Want In Your Life
by Shakti Gawain
Published by Natarj publishing, a division of new World library, Novato California, 2002, 1995,1978
originally Published by Berkeley, Calif Whatever Pub 1978

Tapping the Power Within
A Path to Self- Empowerment for Black Women
By Iyanla Vanzant
Published by Writers and Readers 1992

Psychotherapy 2.0
Where Psychotherapy and Technology Meet
Edited by Philippa Weitz
Published by Karnac book Ltd 2014 and re published by Routledge 2018

Chapter 10 by Aqualma Murray – Protecting Children and Young People – The Online generation.

Printed in the United States
By Bookmasters